Salted with
FIRE

Life-stories, Meditations, Prayers

IAN M FRASER

First published in 1999 by
SAINT ANDREW PRESS
121 George Street, Edinburgh EH2 4YN

Copyright © Ian M Fraser 1999

ISBN 0 7152 0762 8

British Library Cataloguing in Publication Data
 A catalogue record for this book
 is available from the British Library.

  ISBN 07152 0762 8

Cover design by Mark Blackadder.
Cover and internal photographs by Paul Turner.
Typesetting by Lesley A Taylor.
Printed and **bound** in Great Britain by Redwood Books, Trowbridge, Wiltshire.

Salted with FIRE

IAN M FRASER

Salted with Fire

DEDICATION   vi
INTRODUCTION   vii

1   **IN GOD'S WORLD**
        Getting rooted in reality   2
        God is there   14
        Live and learn   22
        Cultural interaction   32
        Tough challenges   42
2   **IN GOD'S CHURCH**
        Renewing Church   58
        Church alive   72
        Basic Christian communities   84
        Biblical resources   94
3   **IN GOD'S ENTERPRISE**
        Dunblane   108
        Breaking barriers   116
        Ecumenical encounters   126
4   **FAITH'S TESTING**
        Troubles and testing   136
        End-game   146

CONTENTS

*To my grandchildren
– the joy they bring me!*

DEDICATION

A T the beginning of Romans 12, Paul urges his readers and hearers to offer their bodies (*ie* their whole beings) as a living sacrifice. Sacrifices offered to God had to be savoury, so salt was normally added. Jesus urges his followers 'be salted with fire'. In his *Natural History*, Pliny observes, 'Salt has something of the nature of fire'. It purges and purifies. Life does that to us. Something like that happened with my wife Margaret and myself over our years together until her death in 1987. What we got involved in had a purifying effect and added savour to the life we shared. Hence the title of this book.

It was Margaret who, conscious of the privilege of the experiences which burnt away a lot of the dross in our lives and at the same time added savour to them, urged me to get some of these stories into print.

I did this in *Strange Fire* (Wild Goose Publications, 1994), adding prayers which, in germ, seemed to be embedded in the experiences. The prayers accompanying the stories in this book are culled from a further range of experiences.

I would like to acknowledge the valued work of John Henderson in processing this material.

Ian M Fraser

INTRODUCTION

1

IN GOD'S WORLD

Getting rooted in reality
God is there
Live and learn
Cultural interaction
Tough challenges

NAMING LOVE

SOMETIMES one's grip on reality needs to be reinforced. Pressure of circumstances can have a distorting effect.

In 1945 my appointment as Scottish Secretary of the SCM involved a move to Edinburgh. We got rooms in a house which had been inhabited by a single family and now accommodated seven couples and singles. Kitchen and bathroom were shared. It was made clear to Margaret and me that children were all right provided they made no noise through the night. We had almost to smother the cries of Anne and, later, Keith. My own job was very demanding – making one company out of returnees from the war and students coming straight from school.

At one point I found myself resenting what amounted to a modest share of childminding. I needed to take myself in hand. A handle on reality took the form of this poem:

> *I love, my dear,*
> *you combing out your hair;*
> *quick, light step in a windswayed frock,*
> *quick needle shining in shirt or sock,*
> *washing, gay on a dancing line,*
> *dance of your eyes as they meet mine:*
> > *wife, witch, lover,*
> > *my joy and crown:*
> > > *eyes whose sympathy soothes so much,*
> > > *voice which, at the dusting, sings,*
> > > *delicate hands whose craftsman touch*
> > > *twines love around the commonest things.*

That kept the real Margaret before me …

PRAYER

God the Lord,
We are called to love you with heart, soul and strength
and our neighbours as ourselves;
to seek first your Kingdom and righteousness –
then, all that matters will be added.
But to give you first place in our lives often defeats us.
Most often we give you the leftovers of energy and time.
For life knocks us around, makes great demands;
people load us with their worries, cares and frustrations;
the demands of work or unemployment keep increasing,
bringing us near breaking point.
People tell us to get a grip on ourselves
but it is your grip on us that we need.
So take a grip on us, Lord,
forgive what we have been, direct what we shall be;
enable us from this day on to give you first place in our lives
and let other things fit in:
some to be discarded, some kept
some given more time, some less
to your praise and glory.
Show your grace to those who seek to build a loving relationship
amid all life's hassles:
that they may invest the time, love, energy, persistence
which provides a secure foundation
and find resources to carry them through difficult times,
remembering how precious it is to love and be loved.
We ask it in the name of him who came
because you love this disordered, stressful world. Amen.

NAMING GOD

SHE had an impish face and a style to match. In the north-east we would have called her 'a bit of a besom'. I took to her from the start. But then I did not have to live with her. The husband who did had either given up the ghost or just given up, leaving her with three children to rear. She seemed to be always trailing around to no visible purpose. When school did not claim them, the children trailed with her, hanging on her arms. It was as if they were closing ranks, happy to be together.

I could not imagine any circumstances which would finally get her down.

On the day in question I knew there was serious business afoot. Instead of calling me by name, she addressed me as 'minister'. The signal was not lost on me. What she confided would not be for any ears, but for mine in my official capacity. At the same time I knew that what she said would not be in the form of a confession. Confessions were not in her line. Her way was to come alongside and share. There would be no mental grill between us.

'It's the kids, minister,' she started. 'They're growin' up fast. I canna haud clothes and meat tae them. I decided I needed a job.

'My sister-in-law worked in a butcher's shop and intended tae leave. She put me up tae the whole thing. She said she would pretend tae be ill. I would tak the message tae the butcher's an' offer tae stand in for her. Efter a week or two she would say she was leavin' for good. By that time I would hae gotten the hang o' things and they wouldna be likely tae look for somebody else.

'It worked like a charm. I'm in the job; things are better for the family. But it wasna' richt, was it, minister? If my sister-in-law had handed in her chips the usual wey, the job would hae been advertised an' somebody else micht hae got it. We werna playin' straicht, were we, minister?

'I wonder what God thinks o't. He'd hae seen through oor game. But he'd ken aboot the kids' needs tae.

'What dae you think, minister? Micht God even hae liked oor cheek – had a guid laugh tae himsel?

'He's a humorous kind o' devil, is he no – God?'

PRAYER

Almighty God, Lord of all,

How refreshing you must find jaunty, harum-scarum, irrepressible humanity, expressing reverence for you irreverently – you who are so often loaded with earnest and sober and wearisome adulation.

How you must relish that security in love which puts guilt aside as a child puts away toys, and nestles trustingly in your arms.

How your eyes must kindle with delight, your feet itch to dance, your voice sing your thankfulness that at times the human spirit, so often unbearable, can also prove to be unbeatable.

How great are the risks you have taken in bringing us into being and trusting us with your world! How marvellous is the love which took those risks! How patiently you have contended with us all through the ages, crucified by our sinfulness, cheered by our resilience.

We bless and praise your glorious name who out of the mouths of babes and besoms have perfected praise; and confess the church's age-long conspiracy to hide your true nature from many
– making you out to be a God who terrorises, letting no sin go unrecorded and unpunished
– or making you remote, defining you by what we are not: omnipotent, omniscient, omnipresent ...
– or making you our jailor who confines us in straightjackets which cramp the generous impulses of the human spirit as if it were not for the joy set before him that Jesus endured the cross when the exodus accomplished at Jerusalem released us into freedom.

Enable us to look twice at ordinary folk
going about the business of life
in whom clues to your nature may reside,
expressed in perceptive common speech,
in Jesus Christ's name. Amen.

CHILDREN NAME THE REAL

WHEN the Dunblane Music Group got into its stride in the 1960s, it soon realised that new hymns for children were needed. Many of the existing ones seemed to be control devices, designed to keep children quiet and well-behaved. Few young people had the creatively rebellious spirit of a daughter of the manse who, faced with the verse:

For we know the Lord of glory
always sees what children do
and is writing down the story
of their thoughts and actions too.

May my sins be all forgiven,
bless the friends I love so well,
take me when I die to Heaven
happy there with thee to dwell,

did the following reconstruction job:

May my friends be all forgiven,
bless the sins I love so well,
save me, when I die, from heaven:
I'd much rather sample Hell.

Traditional hymnwriters had so often fallen into a trap. 'Jesus the child' could be rhymed with 'meek and mild'. The pattern of Jesus' life was transmuted into a device to restrain the behaviour of children! Yet a twelve year old who gave his parents the slip and caused Joseph an extra three day's loss of wages might be more accurately described by the rhyming adjective 'wild'!

In the 1960s Gracie King undertook to get the Bo'ness Music Department pupils to compose and to judge children's hymns. First, the children had to be broken away from the idea that traditional hymns provided good guides. What they then wrote turned out to be very sensuous. What suggested God at work in the world? The feel of smooth stones, the lapping of water, the sound of a well-tuned engine, the sight of a friend coming to greet you.

New hymns written by adults which appealed were laid aside for a month or two. Only if they were asked for again by children were they brought back into play. That sorted out ephemeral appeal from that which spoke to children in a deep and lasting way.

REFLECTION

Let the Holy Spirit fill you. Speak to one another in psalms, hymns and songs; sing and make music from your heart to the Lord: and in the name of our Lord Jesus Christ give thanks every day for everything to our God and Father.

~ Ephesians 5: 18-20 ~

PRAYER

Marvellous and mysterious God the Lord,

You are to be praised with heart and voice, with well-tuned instruments, with words which speak your glory. The dumb creation looks to us to make articulate its longing to be transformed; the human family seeks expression of its thankfulness that you, not evil powers, are finally in charge of life. In psalms, hymns and songs we raise to you doubts and fears, sorrows and sufferings, hopes and expectations, exuberant love of living, the crushing experience of bereavement – there is nothing, no one who cannot be hymned into your presence and blessed.

Forgive us that we have drawn so little on the ability of children to perceive your nature and to put their wonder into words: teach us again that of such is the Kingdom of Heaven.

Put a guard on our lips, we pray: lest we be dumb when we should be magnifying you, lest we use words to cover up reality rather than to expose it, lest we be content with rote repetition void of underlying conviction;

but do you only 'open my lips and my mouth shall show forth your praise'. Let me exalt you in my life, and let the words I find to tell this out be acceptable in your sight,

O Lord, my strength and my Redeemer. Amen.

ACCURATE NAMING

NOT long after Scottish Churches House came into being in 1960, a group of artists used the national press to lambast the churches for alleged philistinism in their attitude to the arts. We invited them to share their concerns with a wider company. They accepted – and found those whom they thought they would be charging against, charging alongside them!

Most of the Glasgow group declared themselves to be at least agnostic about the Christian faith, probably atheistic.

When an excellent transparency of Picasso's 'Guernica' was thrown on the screen at a later consultation, a Christian artist had said,

'There are deep Christian insights in that work.'

Jim Morrison immediately burst out, 'You Christian monopolists! You can't see anything good without trying to get your claws on it and claim it for your own. That is an atheistic statement by a Marxist!'

Jim had gifted to the House a personal painting of Glasgow tenements in which he was brought up. The grimness is there, and also the human spirit shining through. When we returned to Scotland in 1982 the kitchen staff got hold of me: 'We are fed up with that painting at the far end of the dining room: any chance of getting another "Jim Morrison" to replace it?' I phoned Jim just to let him know about their good taste.

Two minutes later he was back on the line. He had consulted his wife. There was a triptych in the National Gallery which might serve the purpose. If it did not, we were not to feel under any obligation either to take it or to retain it. We must not try to pay for it.

He made just one request. When it was opened out, people were asked to reflect – 'The earth is the Lord's and the fullness thereof'; and when it was closed for Lent – 'The grass withereth, the flower fadeth: but the Word of our God shall stand forever.'

It opens up more than the end wall of the dining room!

REFLECTION

Reflect on church traditions which have over-emphasised words, formulae, dogmatic statements to which assent is required. Is there not in this a search for security other than in God? Taken to the limit, are such traditions not blasphemous?

Give thanks for those who, in different media, home in on reality, exposing its creative quality, its frightening possibilities, its profound contradictions – so that our imagination is touched and comfortable stereotypes broken, and we are provided with the incentive to keep journeying into truth.

Give thanks for those who care so much about art that they are prepared to assail establishments which they believe devalue struggles to grasp reality; who when they are met with friendship and candour are prepared to move in their thinking; who graciously remind us of gifts given to the human race through creative exploration in all kinds of fields.

Ask for God's forgiveness for occasions when we ascribe to Christianity what has come from outside its orbit – as if God did not have witnesses outwith the historic faith who can instruct and enlarge it by their testimony, as Wise Men did recognising the Christ-child when those within the tradition were blind.

And bless God for kitchen folk who appreciate true quality when they see it.

PRAYER

Lord of all life,
Enable us to stand, alert and appreciative, before people's gifts, that we may not miss the glory which is reflected over all the earth, from whatever direction and source it comes.
We ask it in your own name. Amen.

PERCEPTIVE YOUTH

IN the 1960s firms sent male apprentices with their Training Officers to Scottish Churches' House. The aim was not to get apprentices and trainers away from industrial concerns on to some 'religious ground'. It was to give them time and space to think more deeply about what they were already doing.

A problem could have been that of discipline. The windows of ground-floor bedrooms gave immediate access to the Cathedral Square. What if the young lads, full of energy, sallied out late at night and into the early hours and 'lit up the town'?

Whatever was done would need to have their clear consent. I put it to them. Staff had a right to time off and sleep. Staff also needed to know that the House had been secured for the night. If they would agree to be within its walls by a time they chose themselves, I would make that the locking-up time. I expected something of the order of one o' clock in the morning to be chosen.

The first suggestion was eleven at night. It was immediately pounced on by the others. Staff had been working all day. They needed time off. Besides, they, the apprentices, could talk as much as they wanted inside the House. Ten or half-ten would be fairer! When I said that I would be perfectly happy with an eleven o' clock closure they treated that as a major concession!

On the occasion of one conference a double-feature James Bond programme was being presented in a Stirling cinema: 'From Russia With Love' and 'Dr No'. A visit was included in the programme. The following day an assessment took place. What did they think of the Bond women? Tongues ran round lips: 'Lush, man, lush.'

'If you had the chance, would you marry one?'

From the whole company, as one, 'Not on your life, sir!'

The biggest and toughest, who had shown himself to be a natural leader, added, 'When I marry, I want somebody like my granny.'

REFLECTION

Let this same mind be in you that was in Christ Jesus,
who, though he was in the form of God
did not regard equality with God as something to be exploited
but emptied himself, taking the form of a slave;
being born in human likeness and found in human form
he humbled himself....   ~ Philippians 2: 5–8 ~

PRAYER

Lord God,
We give you thanks and praise that you know what it is like to be one
of us through Jesus Christ our Lord; for all that flesh was heir to he
was heir to.
>   *We do not need to aspire to an ideal world where life will be*
>   *smoother and we will always be on the winning side, for he*
>   *had his feet on the ground in the real world, faced failure, and*
>   *from that vantage point opened a door of hope to all humanity.*
You allow us our dreams and they can come true.
You allow us our visions and these may fruitfully direct our life.
>   *But it is feet-on-the-ground that we have to live life, with real*
>   *people, in raw contexts, tied in with no means of escape,*
>   *as you, Lord Christ, wrought our salvation, emptied of surreal*
>   *power and glory, knowing human weakness, bearing human*
>   *defeat and pain.*
We give you thanks for young people
>   *who lick their lips over the impossible and choose the real,*
>   *who beneath surface reactions hold to true values*
>   *giving faithfulness in relationships preference over fantasy;*
>   *and give you thanks that there is that in human nature which*
>   *can discount hollow allurements and choose real character in*
>   *those whom they would seek to partner through life.*
Grant us to be feet-on-the-ground Christians, in Christ. Amen.

DEEP SPRINGS

'In quietness and in confidence shall be your strength.'
~ Isaiah 30: 15 ~

IN Zamboanga City, Mindanao, in 1982 we were invited to meet with Carmelite nuns. Margaret and I wondered what to converse about, for they are a contemplative order, 'confined to barracks', concentrating on meditation and prayer. The meeting was memorable on both sides. When later they heard of Margaret's death, they let me know that, every anniversary, they would hold a mass to remember her and rejoice in her life. That day they assembled behind iron bars to meet with us and spoke through the grills.

What struck us, for our part, was their understanding of developments in the Philippines. In the course of our six-week visit we had met with researchers, analysts, social workers, political activists. None seemed to us to have the rounded appreciation of events which the nuns exhibited. We had to deal with a mystery, for these were people shut away from the traffic of humanity. Do some perceptions come through the air to sensitive people? Does prayer provide a kind of chute down which knowledge comes to those ready to receive it, who look to God for light?

The nearest I had come to this phenomenon in previous experience was when I went into industry as a worker-pastor in 1942. I had been judged by some to have wasted my training and ruined any prospects of advancement I had, by doing so. Professor Donald Baillie thought otherwise, and invited me to St Andrews to discuss with his students the significance of the step. He was troubled by severe asthmatic problems. These made him almost a recluse. I doubt if he ever set foot in a factory in his life. Yet he perceived what eluded others.

REFLECTION

How many are the ways in which God's purposes are effected!
People sometimes escape into quiet backwaters, make that a way of evading the world's tough challenges. That defeats God's purposes.
'More things are wrought by prayer ...' – wrought by prayer, not just understood but wrought . People are called to get purchase on the world's life by prayer and turn it in the direction of the Kingdom.

PRAYER

Those of us who are embroiled in the world give thanks to you, Lord God, for those who offer the obedience of withdrawal.
We know that, in fights for justice, we are sustained by their prayers.
We know that, in the confusion of choices which face us, we depend for guidance on those who gain clarity through meditation.
We know that the pressure upon us to act has to be balanced by the need to contemplate.

Those of us who are in some way withdrawn from the world, by choice, by accident or infirmity, give thanks that you accept our offering of prayer and praise.
– We pray that, if there should be in this withdrawal escapism from proper responsibilities, you will reveal this to us, that we may repent and amend our ways.
– We pray that, in measure as we are being truly obedient, that may be a sign to the world that it needs to be more thoroughly steeped in praise and prayer.
In the quiet recesses of the hearts of the active, nourish discernment!
In the projection into the world of fruits of reflection, nourish transformation!
Be exalted, O Lord in your strength! Amen.

PLACES OF PRESENCE

'SURELY the Lord is in this place,' said Jacob at Bethel. He thought he was on foreign territory; and found that what he thought of as alien could be a place of special revelation.

At the time of the founding of the Iona Community, I told myself that I would not be the victim of the romantic responses to the island made by Dr Johnson and others. Iona was an island, no more. The first year I succeeded; the second equally. On my third visit I had to submit. The Lord is in that place! Geography and history combine to refresh and restore, renew and enlarge human life.

St Basil's in the Kremlin, to me, was God's fireworks display – a place of fizzing colourful delight, in the sunshine.

The train from Tokyo to Kyoto kept Mount Fuji steadily in sight. A mountain like any other? No way. An object of superstition? Rather a place of presence.

With a companion I went for a walk in the Shetland Isles. Round a bend, I found a bay stretched beneath us.

'The lively tranquillity of the Celtic church seems to be there,' I ventured.

'That,' said my companion, 'is St Ninian's Bay.'

That lively tranquillity is manifested also in Dunblane where St Blane founded his monastic community in AD 600 or 602. Tourists and buses cannot obliterate it.

PRAYER

Eternal Father,
You bed yourself in time and space.
You have come to us throughout history, since ever beings could be
called human. You have striven with our spirits to mature in us that
humaneness which reflects your likeness.

Yet you chose a particular time to bring to us the full revelation of
your glory. Jesus testified: 'The time is fulfilled and the kingdom of
God has come near; repent and believe the gospel.' Not any time: the
particular time of your favour had come.

You address us in every place where we are to be found. Said the
psalmist: 'If I take the wings of the morning and dwell at the furtherest
limits of the sea, even there your hand shall lead me and your right
hand shall hold me.' Yet you chose one spot on the earth to bring to
us the full revelation of your glory – a small place, crushed between
empires.

We give you thanks that there are places which make it easier for
us to meet you. In homes made redolent of your presence by the
love of those who live there. In caves and on mountain tops. Before
burning bushes or fields aflame with summer flowers. In places
where prayer seems to impregnate walls. In trysting places where we
meet one another in your presence and discover a love deep-rooted
in yours.

We pray for those whose every place, in home, in neighbourhood,
in pub and disco, is restless with noise and disturbance; and also for
those who use the loud beat of background music as a relaxing aid
for establishing friendship.

Teach us to seek, for all people, environments which enable true
relationships to flourish.

We ask it in Jesus Christ's name. Amen.

JESUS MAKES HIMSELF PRESENT

FROM the moment she arrived in the hall where the Jumble Sale was held, people gave her a wide berth. A pong hung about her like an aura and marked her passage wherever she went. It seemed to me to be compounded of strong body sweat, a hint of confined space and children's sick. I imagined her occupying a single room with children and no partner to help, without decent washing facilities, just managing to survive one day at a time.

She seemed to have given up on the possibility of being treated with respect. She looked neither to left or right and was greeted by no one. Clutching a big, empty bag she made straight for the children's clothes stall. Instead of taking up garments singly, she took them in fistfuls, enquiring the price. The stallholder, probably moved by a mixture of compassion and hope that she would not linger, named a low figure. She stuffed them in her bag, paid, and went straight out of the door, again looking neither to left nor right.

I had kept clear too.

I had just crossed the Bristol Road to go to my office in Selly Oak when the man stopped me and asked directions. He was looking for a road or street which he believed to be in the vicinity. His was a narrow, pale, malnourished face in which the bones stuck out. At the corners of his eyes were flecks of green pus and there was green snot at his nose. I said I was sorry, I had no knowledge of the place he was looking for, that the name meant nothing to me; and went on my way. It was then that he threw after me, 'I was only asking a civil question'.

Had I turned away too quickly? Had I shown some revulsion? I could have paused for a moment or two, called on the assistance of another passerby. He might then at least have felt affirmed. As it was, he clearly felt rejected.

I had met Jesus Christ in a woman and a man, Jesus of the Smells, Jesus of the Snot. I had been taken off guard: had not even spared Jesus the time of day.

PRAYER

Lord God,
We bless you that those who have seen Jesus Christ have seen you.
If at times we think of you radiating that glory which made Moses
and Elijah veil their faces lest they be dazzled and blinded by it,
teach us also to think of you present as Christ among the crowds which
daily mill all around us. Remind us that in him you identified yourself
with those counted lowest and least on this world's reckoning.
He knew the smell of the poor, mewed up in malodorous slums,
lacking space, lacking water, often lacking hope for anything better.
He knew the incessant noise from which the poor suffer; and heard
in their cries, prayers for help.
He laid his hand healingly on the disfigured and diseased,
touching them to life.
He revelled in the feasts of the poor; and refused drugged wine
on the cross.
He saw in discarded humanity the potential of children of God –
and so redeemed our senses – smell, hearing, touch, taste, sight:
enabling us to employ them for the transformation of life rather than
merely for our own satisfactions.
If you ask it, give us the grace to exchange the sweet airs of hill-
sides for the fetid air of slums;
the quiet of the study for the din of overcrowded quarters;
protected health for exposure to humanity's unhealed infections;
loaded shelves for minimum rations.
Train our eyes to see in every person the Christ whom we are
called to serve.

Make us anew in your image, Lord Christ;
redeem all our senses; show us what you want of our life.
Teach us to look at reality unflinchingly and see you at its heart lest
your beloved children feel, when they look at us,
that you are absent from your world.
In your own name we ask it. Amen.

PRESENCE VEILED

IN my time, divinity students in Edinburgh could offer service in New College Settlement, the Pleasance, as part of their training for ordained ministry. The area, since then redeveloped, was run down.

What stays with me from that time is two pairs of eyes.

A variety of services were offered by the Settlement. We conducted worship, took part in debates and discussions, prepared and presented concerts for the enjoyment of the locals and ourselves, and undertook responsibilities for visiting in the area.

On this occasion I climbed stairs, knocked at a door, was told to come in. The couple, like wizened apples, were sitting on chairs as if they had been stuck in them for the whole day. The floor was bare. There was almost no other furniture. A small fire burned in the grate. Glazed eyes took me in as if I were not there.

I attempted conversation. They gave short, uninterested answers. It was as if they had given up on life altogether, had lost interest in trying to make anything of it. Had they had children who had died or gone to the bad? Had they some other incapacitating secret sorrow? Had they been beaten in the struggle to make ends meet, to get sufficient food, to keep warm? They seemed dislocated from any sense of hope, prepared to sit dumbly from day to day from morning till night, to do nothing else. Nothing mattered. Nothing at all mattered. I could make no headway.

Half a century later, lacklustre eyes stay with me. They harboured no reproof. They exist as a reproof.

REFLECTION

Jesus Christ came that all might have life,
life more abundant.

PRAYER

Lord Christ,
You showed us how we should live and serve.
You spread hope wherever you went; preaching the Kingdom –
the whole fabric of the created life shaped according to the Father's
purpose;
healing the sick, giving sight to the blind, making the lame walk,
curing the deaf and dumb; teaching the way we should live –
loving God and loving our neighbour as ourselves.

You said, 'Greater things than these shall you do because I go to the
Father'.

We confess that we continually let you down and let others down.
Instead of the 'greater things'
– we allow systems to stay in place which create wealth for some
and poverty for others, depriving both of true life in different ways;
– we allow people to be labelled successes or failures, ignoring a
whole range of qualities for living which 'failures' possess, since
they are made in your image;
– we do not 'resist unto blood, striving against sins' of homelessness
and poor housing, which make so many sleep rough and lead to
illness and despair: so that people lose life who were born for life
abundant.
Forgive the hurt we cause, often unconsciously, simply by being
preoccupied with our own affairs or failing to persist in the claims
which your love and justice lay upon us.
For only you, who suffers with the sufferers, can, from the depths of
their injury, cleanse us of our sin and enable us to amend our life.
We give thanks that, in you, we are given a fresh chance.
We take hold of the new life you offer.
Enable us, we pray, to play our part in ensuring that the eyes of your
beloved family are kept bright with hope.
We ask it in your own name. Amen.

FLOWER POWER

ON the anniversary of the Warrington bombing, I was in Dublin. Passing a park I realised that flowers and wreaths were being banked high in a protected space near a gate, and I turned aside to investigate. Two attendants in official uniform were taking the flower offerings and laying them out. I asked the nearer one, 'What do you think this means?' He responded without hesitation: 'Those responsible for that outrage said that they were acting on behalf of the people. This is the people making it clear to them that they reject any idea that it was in their name that that violence was perpetrated.'

In 1991 I had been at the University of Bucharest on the second anniversary of the fall of the Ceaucescu dictatorship. Buildings around were pockmarked by bullets. Lives had been lost. The road in front of the university was taken up with students haranguing the crowds, urging them to use the freedom which was now theirs. To get the necessary space for meeting, the roads had had to be blocked off. The students laid a line of flowers to exclude traffic. Not one car, not one heavy lorry even put a tyre on that fragile barrier.

It stays vividly in my mind, that poster at the time of the Vietnam War of the girl confronting the soldier – a gun in his hand, a flower in hers. I feel also for the young, bewildered serviceman caught in that system.

PRAYER

Lord God, shall the meek really inherit the earth?
Did you choose what is foolish in the world to shame the wise;
what is weak in the world to shame the strong;
what is low and despised in the world, even things which are not,
to reduce to nothing things that are –
so that none may boast in your presence?
Then blessed be your glorious name
and let the whole world be filled with your glory.
But we have a long way to go. Forgive us that
– we trust in our own power, our own persuasiveness, our capacity
to overbear others and get our way, even when we are supposed
to be witnessing to your way of grace;
– we do not want to be foolish, weak, low and despised nothings,
forgetting that Jesus Christ made himself 'a nothing'* to identify
himself with human existence.
How can you ever make us see life the way you do?
We acknowledge that power-play cannot sustain a fostered image
of being an instrument for righteousness. The grain of the universe
runs with the concerns of the Kingdom not with the goals of the
selfish and powerful.
Yet there is much in human nature which is brutal and degrading.
Neighbours turn on neighbours to rape and kill. Our natures need
to be changed utterly. But it takes more than natural goodness to pro-
duce that change.
So enter into our beings, Lord Christ, not to overwhelm us but to
release those forces in us which are on the side of righteousness –
which engender right relationships, right actions, life put right side
up, for,
for this you came and died and rose again
for this you share your life with us in the eucharist.
We ask this in order that the world at last may become the world of
your promise ... in which the flower faces down the gun. Amen.

[**doulos:* a slave or a nothing (Philippians 2: 7)]

THE WEDDING

IT was my first wedding as an ordained minister, in 1948.

I was waiting outside Rosyth Parish Church, glad to have Mr Ross, the senior elder, with me. For it is one thing to know almost by heart what the book says, quite another to conduct a ceremony as important as this so that it is meaningful for the parties concerned and still does what the law requires.

While waiting for the wedding foursome to turn up, we became aware of a man in the telephone box across the road who was speaking into the mouthpiece and looking across in our direction. Eventually he crossed the road, came up to us and declared, 'I have authority to stop this wedding!'

The lines of authority and legal niceties are matters one learns to cope with, with experience. All my experience lay in the future. But I asked, 'Whose authority?' 'The bride's parents,' came the reply – 'they have just been on the phone authorising me to act for them.' I said, 'We'll check that once the bride and groom turn up.'

Shortly afterwards they did. Mr Ross and I examined their papers. The banns of marriage had been legally and publicly displayed in the bride's parish. There was no impediment to our proceeding with the marriage. So I went ahead.

We had just attended to the signing of the official documents in the vestry when the bride's parents turned up. Her father was a big miner who had had an accident in the pit. One leg was in plaster which came up to near the waist. Finding that the deed was done, the bride's mother stepped forward, slapped the bridegroom viciously on the side of the face and fell in a faint at his feet. At that, the bride's father took a step forward and punched the bridegroom on the chin.

I had not been led to believe that these were necessary accompaniments to the sealing of the marriage bond. But, as I said, experience to match theory with practice lay ahead at that point of my life.

Shortly afterwards I took care to investigate how things had worked out. The bride and groom were settled happily – in the home of the bride's parents!

PRAYER

God of all life,
   We meet you as the Giver of Law, of 'Torah', the Teaching, the
   How-to-Live.
   We meet you as the loving Father and Mother of us all.
   We bless you that you who are both of these are also one.

Thanks and praise are your due
that there are laws, regulations, guidelines, codes of practice which
serve to restrain those human tendencies which would fashion life in
a way which is unfair or which serves selfish purposes;
and there are laws which protect people from oppression and
exploitation and free them to make a creative use of their lives.
–   Forgive us for laws which allow the powerful to subdue the weak;
–   Nerve us to fight to replace these with laws which serve your justice.

Thanks and praise are your due
for love which goes beyond all laws and regulations, which spends
itself sacrificially, which never stops loving even if faced with rejection
and scorn.
We give thanks for your boundless love; and that you respect our
need for space; that instead of unveiling your awesome majesty and
forcing us to conform, you remain invisible, waiting on our response.
–   Forgive us that we fill so much of the space which your love pro-
   vides with the violation of human lives instead of with their
   cherishing: as if you were not only invisible but absent.
–   Turn us, we pray, to your ways, your loving, life-giving ways.

Hear us for young people reaching adulthood and their parents, that
they may learn together the freedom of law and the restraints of love:
remembering ....
Hear us for those caught in a cleft stick, unclear about what law and
love demand, remembering dilemmas with which
.... and .... are faced.

In Jesus Christ's name. Amen.

THE BLIND SEE

A WORKFORCE of blind people in Hong Kong felt driven to the point where they had to do something more drastic about their situation than just protest verbally to the management. They lacked job security. Their wages were low. The administration seemed to them to be unsympathetic. A change of policy was under consideration which could make the workshop operate on a more impersonal basis. They went on strike, and turned to an ecumenical team for support. The Hong Kong Christian Industrial Committee placed before the public, through its *Workers' Weekly*, the facts which other papers would not publish. Representatives from the Committee, with Roman Catholics – who had been the first to act – formed a support group.

The temptation to take over the situation must have been strong. Blind people have a look of helplessness. The sighted may forget that they have all their wits about them. This worked out as an 'alongside' operation. The initiative was left with the blind workers. They decided to march the streets to bring the attention of the public to their cause – the support group simply saw to it that they kept clear of traffic. They decided to hold a sit-in: the support group enabled them to carry through their decision, taking in blankets and food, and leading people to the toilet, and so on. About 200 took up strategic stances at the Star Ferry, and raised $50,000 (Hong Kong) for a fighting fund; the support team helped them to find the right kind of lawyers.

To be present at a meeting of the Strategic Planning Committee was to realise the new vitality possessed by the blind workers, helped by an awareness that, backed by others, they could fight their own battles and fight them successfully.

REFLECTION

*As he was getting into the boat, the man who had been possessed
by demons begged him that he might stay with him. But Jesus
refused and said to him: 'Go home to your friends and tell
them how much the Lord has done for you and what mercy he
has shown you.' And he went away and began to proclaim in
the Decapolis how much Jesus had done for him: and everyone was amazed.* ~ Mark 5: 18-20 ~

*Jesus not only cured, he healed. Wholeness included the restoration
of the capacity for initiative which the demoniac had lost. It was
disciples, not dependents, whom Jesus drew around him. They came
to maturity not when they echoed his teaching but when they made it
their own.*

PRAYER

– *Pray for politicians who make the fear of encouraging 'dependency' (which they have created through their own policies) an
excuse for giving society's discards much less than their share of
those resources which God has provided for all.*
– *Pray for those thrown into dependency from birth through no fault
of their own; denied adequate food, shelter, education, health-
care.*
– *Pray for those who twist words to classify as 'workshy',
'parasites'; those who were denied the chance to show initiative.*

*Ask God that we may all learn to be parts of a body, each one
significant, each depending on the other, building one another up in
love;*
*ask forgiveness for any way in which you have patronised the
differently-abled or turned from them as if you owed them nothing,
when Jesus Christ is in them, longing to bless you.*
Ask it in his name. Amen.

DAILY MIRACLES

I HAVE seen a wonder. I have seen it again and again in different parts of the planet. To me it is one of the great wonders of the world. I have seen boys and girls turned out with fresh clean shirts and blouses day after day from shacks and hovels.

I have experienced a wonder. I have experienced it again and again in different parts of the planet. To me it is one of the great wonders of the world. I have experienced people with virtually nothing to live on who scrape from somewhere the means to enable families to survive for just one more day at a time, and still care for their neighbours. I have lived with them and their persisting hope has taken my breath away.

These are often looked on as inarticulate. In fact to act as they do is to articulate, by their way of tackling life rather than by words, a deep theological perception. To turn out children immaculate from a slum is a statement that they are made in the image of God and should look the part. To edge one's life and that of one's neighbours through one more day successfully is a statement that life matters, that it is a gift of God to be cherished and won continually from destructive forces.

An imaginative reporter, finding a promising young footballer tongue-tied when he interviewed him, observed, 'Where he is articulate is on the field of play'.* It is not in a language of words but of life that many people articulate deep convictions.

We should be humble and teachable before the poor. But we should not be content that they stay poor to show what God's grace can achieve. For them there is little of the life abundant – which Jesus Christ came to secure for all. I think of a pedlar husband, wife and children in Lima, Peru. The children would have been about five and seven years. They all had to work from morning till night to scrape enough together to survive for one more day. Life abundant was not for them. Yet Jesus Christ came to put it on offer.

[*Have you ever noticed how articulate Ginger Rogers' feet are, when she dances with Fred Astaire?]

REFLECTION

*He has shown strength with his arm,
he has scattered the proud in the imaginations of their hearts;
he has brought down the powerful from their thrones
and exalted the lowly;
he has filled the hungry with good things
and sent the rich empty away.*
~ Magnificat, Luke 1: 51-53 ~

PRAYER

God our Father,
*We need very different eyes if we would see things as you do. We
see and see – and don't see, as Jesus said. We regard people with rank
and honours as special, but your special love is for those denied rank
and honour, denied that dignity which they are due through being
created in your likeness.*

*Forgive our blindness, we pray; and enlighten our eyes that we may
see people as you see them, and appreciate the quality of their lives.*
God the Son,
*You consorted with those whom society marginalised. Yet often we
choose to be found alongside those with power and status.*

*Forgive our false choices, we pray. Open our eyes that we may
see the poor as our instructors concerning the Kingdom and its true
priorities.*
God the Spirit,
*You strive with human spirits to get people to realise their true
stature. When they are almost broken and defeated by circumstances,
you put a light in their eyes, a spring in their step, resolution in their
approach to life. You help us all to become what we truly are.*

*Forgive our defeatism, we pray – as if we had not prayed. 'Your
kingdom come, Your will be done on earth as in heaven'. Teach us,
through the poor, fresh determination to seize life and make the most
of it because it is your gift.*

Trinity of love and power, *We ask this in your name. Amen.*

TRUSTING THE STRANGER

IN visiting countries which were new to me, to carry out the World Council of Churches' Participation in Change programme, I found it necessary to establish fall-back positions. Often little enough information was available in Geneva about my main constituency, namely poor people who, against the odds, were becoming agents of change because of some resource they found in the Christian faith. I would extract what I could from research into the region, from people of the area in question who visited the Ecumenical Centre and from colleagues who knew that part of the world. But I would also identify one or two people who had their fingers on the pulse of the land and would know what was developing in it. It did not matter whether they were Christian.

The practice served me particularly well when I landed in Abidjan, seeking to make contact with the movements of the Spirit in the Ivory Coast. My Methodist host examined the leads I had identified back in Geneva and declared them to be worthless. I phoned the two fall-back addresses I had taken with me. The occupants were both at home and willing to receive me. They identified two areas of dynamic development (*centres d'animation*). Within hours of landing I was on my way to one of these – Bouaké.

As my custom was, I looked for local, reasonably-priced transport. It turned out to be a big car, designed for six passengers into which double that number crammed. I was the only white person travelling that way. Jammed tightly against me was a woman with a child who would be about three or four years old. There was no seat for him. He became fractious. To my surprise (because of his age) his mother breast-fed him until he calmed down and became sleepy.

At that point without a word she took off her headgear, made a nest of it on my lap, rested her son's head there and stretched him out to sleep between us.

Thank you, unknown woman, for honouring a stranger with a wordless, gracious gesture of trust.

REFLECTION

Out of his full store have all received grace upon grace;
for while the law was given through Moses, grace and truth came
through Jesus Christ. ~ John 1: 16, 17 ~

When those who do not possess the law carry out its precepts by the
light of nature then, although they have no law, they are their own law.
~ Romans 2: 14 ~

PRAYER

Father, Son and Holy Spirit,
all kinds of people are made in your likeness,
all kinds of people are touched by your redeeming and illuminating
power,
all kinds of people are spiritually enlarged.
Only you can say who affirms and responds to you, for people
often do not know themselves what moves them.
Forbid that we discriminate between members of your beloved
human family.
Make our lives open to signs of that grace and truth which speak
of Jesus Christ's presence among all his people.
Make us grateful that, in expected and surprising places, these
qualities shine forth.
We give thanks,
for those who, by straight and truthful speech, help us to face
situations honestly
... for those who make themselves humanly available to share
what knowledge they have and give what advice they can to
travellers on life's journeys;
... for those who have the gift, with or without words, to make the
gracious gesture which treats a stranger as a trusted companion.
Father, Son and Holy Spirit,
may grace and truth so mark the life of your church that all human-
ity may look to you for life and the whole creation offer its praise.
We ask it in the name of Jesus Christ. Amen.

CHEERFUL HELPERS

IN the Bungsipsee area of Chayapoon province in Northern Thailand, I had participated in a Buddhist/Christian work camp. Thereafter I wanted to make my way to Vientiane, Laos to spend some days with daughter Anne, her husband and family before returning home. The leaders of the work camp looked at maps and shook their heads. There was no direct road or rail access from where we were. I would need to return to Bangkok and start again from there.

That procedure would eat into the few days I had to spare. I had noticed that small Datsun vans carried people and goods from one village to another. So I asked the Thais to list on paper about six places along a route which led to Vientiane directly.

From market-place to market-place I went, at each one showing my list and being taken to a van which was going in the right direction. We all had the greatest fun. The Thais were delighted at this eccentric foreigner who did not have a word of their language but trusted in their help and was prepared to be squashed on an inside bench along with other villagers, bags of rice, baskets of vegetables, crates of hens and ducks and other goods. Not once, at the listed stopping places along the way, did they ask me to sit on the roof of the van with a few who shared the space with crates and baskets! They were scrupulous about the amount of money they took. I seemed to be charged about the same as a sack of rice at each stage!

Nong Khai was reached in record time. I crossed the Mekong by ferry, and got full value from the available days with the family.

One is your Master, even Christ,
and you are all brothers and sisters.
~ Matthew 23: 8 ~

No one lives to himself and no one dies to himself.
~ Romans 14: 7 ~

PRAYER

Lord Christ,

Without you we would be at odds with one another. It is because we look to you that we can show grace to one another.

We bless you for mutual availability, readiness to help, good humour and bantering which accompanies assistance, scrupulousness about taking fair payment – which meet us at every turn of the road. We know that the church was meant to be a sign to others of true comradeship.

- *forgive us for our lack of generosity especially to people with strange needs who might take up time, energy, money;*
- *forgive us for looking for credit for what we do, we who are unprofitable servants;*
- *forgive us for joylessness in our journeying.*

We who should be a light to others have fallen down on our vocation. By your forgiveness restore us as a church family so that we can be a blessing to the world family, we pray.

Lord Christ,

You have tied us together in one bundle of life. Let us not act as if we are self-sufficient, neither needing others nor owing them anything.

For the breath of life itself and lungs to use it, we depend utterly on you.

For food, shelter, work, leisure we depend also on one another.

- *forgive us as a church when we keep ourselves to ourselves;*
- *forgive us when we seek the company of the like-minded rather than of those who are asking, seeking, knocking;*
- *forgive us when we make the gospel a sedative for our comfort rather than life for the world;*
- *forgive us when we are unwilling to spend ourselves to help humanity journey to its true goal*

By your forgiveness make us grateful that you travel with us and grateful for others, fellow-pilgrims through life;

and to you be the glory for ever. Amen.

ON CULTURAL SENSITIVITY

IT was in Bungsipsee in the Chayapoon Province of North East Thailand that I joined a work camp of students whose main task was to work with the inhabitants of four villages to secure dependable water supplies by building concrete tanks in which water could be stored. The initiative for the project was developed by Roman Catholics, but the majority of the participants were Buddhist.

We had the usual chores to do in addition to the main tasks. I was sitting in a room which served as a kitchen, preparing vegetables, when a student came in and asked if I had seen another member of the team. I replied that he had been in and had just gone out again. 'In which direction?' asked my questioner. Both my hands were occupied with the vegetables, so I stuck out my foot towards the door and said, 'He went through there.'

I was unaware at that point what the gesture would imply. The foot is not only physically the lowest part of the body. It is considered to be the lowest in status. It was a demeaning thing to give my questioner an answer by means of a movement of the foot. I can imagine the dilemma faced by my hosts. Here is a foreigner who does not seem to know the first thing about what matters and what does not in our culture. Yet he is one of us and works as part of the team. How can we gently put him right?

They found a way next morning. The centre of the notice board was occupied by a cartoon. It showed a gullible-looking white man pointing with one foot. That foot had been drawn big enough to occupy the same space as the whole of the rest of the body.

I got the message.

PRAYER

Father, Son and Holy Spirit,

How you must rejoice in one another, the different parts you play giving relish to the relationship, the unity which you enjoy thus made rich and rewarding. How lively must be your interchanges! How fascinating the deep perceptions you share!

And you have one another to turn to, to lean on, to draw strength from when the cross placed at the heart of life rends your soul.

'O the depth of the riches and wisdom and knowledge of God!'

You have made your universe mysterious, with a great variety of life and with an extraordinary coherence, as if to mirror the colourfulness and concord of your own life. You have made your human family diverse in their historical experiences, in racial, cultural, sexual characteristics, daring them to respond to your life by using their differences as gifts which all may share and rejoice in, till all attain a unity like your own.

We confess that we, who are heirs to such a promise, have let you down.

We have made selfish use of this planet, extracting raw materials without sufficient concern for one another's needs, for our children's children, for wild and domestic animals and birds, for plants and trees – all put in our care to cherish, as trustees acting in your name.

We have dealt insensitively with other races, cultures, histories; and have not honoured the gift of different sexual tendencies: and so have impoverished life.

Forgive us, we pray, and restore us to that true, human state which we have seen in Jesus Christ.

We give thanks for those who correct our crudeness, especially those who do so with humour and good grace.

Make us teachable before you and before one another that we may live truly and be a blessing to your creation and the people who inhabit it.

We ask it in Jesus Christ's name.   Amen.

LIVING LOGIC

IN the West we describe as 'logical' a clear way of arguing step-by-step from a starting point to a conclusion. But only the intellect is engaged. Life is larger.

I was one of three members of the first World Council of Churches' delegation to Cuba. Our first assignment was a conference of Protestant churches. The programme put the opening session at 8 pm. At that hour people were going around finding friends they had not seen for some time, hugging them and getting up to date with news. By 8.30 they were introducing them to new members. By 9 pm a trickle of participants began to move towards the hall. Somewhere between 9.15 and 9.30 the 8 pm session started.

Was that not a logical way to start conferring *as a community*?

At the start of a conference in West Africa, I had to check on the programme – for the first two sessions seemed to bear no relationship to it! It was as if participants prowled around on the edges of the subject, giving voice to their own concerns and insights, seemingly regardless of their relevance. But when they homed in on the theme, I realised that it was now with a richness of understanding of where they all stood, which the first two sessions had provided.

Was it not logical to identify 'rations for the road ahead' before starting a journey together ?

In a consultation at the Orthodox Academy in Crete, I was part of a working group which also had two Chinese members. At the end the leader gave an indication of what might be conveyed to plenary and asked if that represented fairly the mind of the group. No one demurred. But when the report was given one of the Chinese rose up in wrath, protesting, 'You have not listened to the silence of the Northern Chinese!' For them, silence indicated that the report was not acceptable.

Is it not logical to listen to people's silence as well as their speech?

PRAYER

Lord Christ,
During your earthly life you encountered people who were sure of
themselves and of their own way of thinking. They constructed frames
of reference into which others were supposed to fit. You did not fit.
They rejected you
- *you, the religious misfit, who insisted that the Sabbath and*
  other regulations should serve human need, not the other way
  round;
- *you the medical misfit who would not keep clear of people*
  with contagious diseases;
- *you the social misfit who sought out for company society's*
  rejects;
- *you the breaker of racial and sexual prejudices, sharing insights*
  with the Samaritan at the well, prepared to be instructed by a
  Syro-Phoenician woman.

To you, people of all kinds could come, be welcomed, respected,
understood.

God the Lord,
Who showed us how we should treat one another through your
Son's way with us:
- *make us teachable before all ways of thinking and relating*
  which genuinely seek to get to the truth, however strange they
  may appear at first sight;
- *help us to take time to absorb and appreciate the cultures*
  among us which are often devalued, such as those of travellers
  and gypsies and young people:

lest we make our little faith the measure by which others are judged
when judgment belongs to you
to whom be glory for ever. Amen.

AN INSTRUCTIVE CUSTOM

IN 1994 I visited a member of the Iona Community who was pastor in the reservation of Hoopa Indians, in North Carolina.

A custom which I came across showed discernment about the nature of mourning. Not that a reasoned case was made for it. People just seemed to have fallen into the habit. But it was a sure instinct which led them there.

When a graveside service takes place in the West, we leave it to the gravediggers to cover the coffin and restore the earth to its original state. Not so the Hoopa. First the closest relatives take up shovels and put clods of earth on top of the coffin. Then more distant relatives take their turn. Finally friends and neighbours complete the job.

Consider what this can mean to the people most closely affected:
– The thud of clods of earth on a coffin will help bring home to people that a break has taken place in life. It can never be again what it was before. Different terms will need to be accepted for living it. Some part of a family, of a community, has gone, never ever to be replaced.
– It can be a loving thing to clothe a body with earth. It can be thought of as akin to wrapping a shawl round a baby to keep it warm and safe.
– It must surely help people in their grieving.

With us, grieving is mainly a mental process. With the Hoopas it is a total process. Not only do thoughts accompany the body into the earth. The whole being, mental, physical, spiritual is engaged in accepting the reality of death – even warming to it as a possible constructive element in the way all human life is to be lived.

PRAYER

Heavenly Father,
You give us a measure of days. Then one day you say, 'Enough'.
We 'die like beasts', says the psalmist. We are part of the natural order
of creation. We are threatened by its hazards and a prey to its corrup-
tion. You meant it to be so. We are strangers and sojourners on the
earth. Here we have no lasting home.
But we are chosen by you to play our part in transforming life;
we are not only like the beasts but in the likeness of you, our God:
and in the end we will have to report back to you.
Have mercy, we pray, on all who go into your presence to account
for the life they have lived. Have mercy, good Lord.

Lord Christ,
You assailed death, the last enemy. You did it for us, that death
might have no more dominion over us.
Now that we have experienced freedom we did not have before,
– let it not be a freedom to go our own ways – for our life was
bought at a price:
– let it be a freedom to fulfil the promise of the life entrusted to us
that we may, at the end, hear your 'Well done'.

Holy Spirit of God,
You console spirits which are numb with grief.
You comfort us about the past and turn us toward the future
With flaming fire you burn away the dross of our natures
and make us ready for new things.
So, as we are born, journey, die, let us see the seasons of our life
and of the lives of our dear ones
as times of health and hope and harvest
every part of which can speak your praise.
And to you Father, Son and Holy Spirit be all glory
both now ... and for ever. Amen.

TOURISM: THE TWO-EDGED ... ???

ALTHOUGH it was not in my job description when I went to work for the World Council of Churches in Geneva, I was asked as an additional mandate to look into the good and bad effects of tourism on the world scene. My very first conference was on that subject. It was held in the Tutzing Academy, Germany, at the time of the 1969 Munich Oktoberfest.

Unforgettable was the contribution of Rumba Mulia who worked in the tourist industry in Bali. She spoke of the brash way in which world culture, based on western assumptions, impacted on the culture of her land. When traditional dramas were staged it was not uncommon for camera-clickers to step over actors at the front of the stage to get shots of what was going on at the back. The development of the story which the drama presented seemed to matter little. The dramas themselves were originally presented as offerings to the gods. Now they were made offerings to tourists. What did that make tourists?

She went on to say that she would not want Bali culture to be ring-fenced and preserved in its traditional state. 'It contains too much superstition which needs to be shaken out. The dominating culture could do a useful job in helping this to happen. But it would need to change its approach from the abrasive one we are experiencing. It has the means to question features of our culture. But it is we, not outsiders, who should decide what must be kept and what allowed to disappear.

'What is needed is a kindly, thoughtful interplay of cultures which respect one another. Then we can fasten on essentials; and a powerful, proud culture which could swamp ours could instead minister to our healing, and at the same time imbibe some of the grace of living we can make as our contribution.'

PRAYER

God the Lord,
>   *You revelled in extravagance !*
>   *Just as birds and animals were decked out in all the colours of*
> *the rainbow, human communities were variegated in their diversity.*
>   *We praise you for the myriad cultures which adorn your world*
> *and the subcultures which nourish them; and that the way we go*
> *about life is affected by our different environments, histories, tastes,*
> *relationships, forms of speech: issuing in myriad flavours of words, of*
> *inherited attitudes, of communal activities, of music, dramas, dances*
> *– which put a stamp on our ways of life, making them distinctive*
> *and precious.*
>   *We ask your forgiveness that so many cultural heritages have*
> *been devalued or eliminated, whose contribution would have*
> *enhanced the life of the world.*
> *–   especially we confess the brash impact of colonialism,*
> *rubbishing art which it did not understand, as in Benin;*
> *destroying ways of life which it did not appreciate, as with*
> *Aborigines;*
> *taking no action to prevent forest pygmies being enslaved;*
> *allowing to die forms of life in which it saw no profit for itself –*
> *eliminating, eliminating, eliminating people and their creative*
> *works.*
> *Give us perceptiveness, we pray, about the opportunities that the*
> *impact of tourism may afford,*
> *that eyes may be opened to appreciate features of life which were*
> *previously unfamiliar*
> *that all may learn to relate sensitively to new and strange ways*
> *and so be instructed in true living.*

> *All this we ask in the name of Jesus Christ our Lord. Amen.*

SEEING AND DOING

IN 1970 I first visited South Africa. For part of the time Bishop Zulu took me under his wing and at one point introduced me to a remarkable Afrikaner farmer. He showed me three forms of agricultural production, exhibited in his fields.

One demonstrated increased productivity which could be achieved using only the tools already available in that area, if these were employed to maximum effect.

A second showed better results which could be obtained by a careful examination of types of soil, a modest use of particular types of fertiliser and appropriate methods of handling the land (*eg* contour ploughing).

The third form was one in which more advanced technology could be called on – small tractors and seeding machines, for instance.

'In this area,' he explained, 'there is a good agricultural school which the children of farmers can attend once they have finished whatever formal schooling is available. There they will learn all the things which I have demonstrated to you today. But when they go back to work the family land they will tackle it exactly as they did before. If you were able to say "Now, if you took this or that alternative approach …", they would stop you and say "such and such an approach would produce such and such results, another approach these different results". They have it all up here …' – and he tapped his forehead – 'but it is classroom stuff, given at a theoretical level, and that is where it stays.

'There needs to be something before their eyes, not in an exercise book or on a blackboard. They are shown here practical options for the way they may handle the earth.'

He tapped his forehead again: 'If you just get it up here, that does not mean that you get it.'

REFLECTION

*Be doers of the word and not hearers only who deceive themselves ....
Those who look into the perfect law, the law of liberty, and persevere,
being not hearers who forget but doers who act – they will be blessed
in their doing.*   ~ James 1: 22, 25 ~

*For biblical writers God was found to be no static deity but an on-the-
job creator in whose very nature it was to invite the collaboration of
human beings. So to know God was not just an exercise of the mind
but a risk undertaken by the total being. Either we are drawn into
that process of transformation of life-as-is and given a share in the
total work or we remain unenlightened. We cannot know God and
stay where and as we are.*

*Similarly to call on the name of the Lord is to invite God to enter
dynamically into situations which confront us. Consequences for the
use of our lives, whether welcome or unwelcome, will be part of the
package.*

PRAYER

Almighty God,

*We bless you that you are, by your very nature, a being who
interferes for our good. You do not stay detached. You concern yourself with our human lot. You concern yourself with the destiny of
your whole creation. This is the Lord's doing and it is marvellous in
our eyes.*

*Yet we confess that we would often want you to be a distant God,
remote from our struggles, who leaves us to go our own way. We kick
against the pricks at times, for your demands go as deep as your
promises.*

*Yet to know you is life and not to know you is death. Turn us to
yourself, we pray. Give us true knowledge.*

*We ask it in the name of him whose yoke is easy and whose burden
is light. Amen.*

A STRIKE AND ATONEMENT

ON one occasion at Selly Oak Colleges I had a group of about a dozen mature students with varying backgrounds with whom to develop an exercise designed to help them get theological resources for issues faced in the world.

Each was asked for a brief description of a living situation. They then chose to work on that given by a nurse. She came from an evangelical background. In the laundry of the hospital where she worked the staff had gone on strike. She had felt vaguely that her faith required her to do something about this, but she did not know what. She wanted some help. So we stripped down the situation to find … (a) what factors came into the development which preceded strike action; (b) pressures falling on those involved; (c) effects on human relationships; (d) major shaping powers at work; and looked for … (e) 'entry points' or 'handles' which might provide some concrete leverage on events.

We then examined the main policies promoted or advocated, identified values underlying these; and laid an alternative biblical/ theological basis for action. We worked on policies consonant with that basis; on action to implement these; and finally checked on the relevance and realism of our proposals.*

When the others left, the nurse stayed behind. Her face was radiant. 'I thought I had to do something about that strike,' she said. 'I have also been attracted by and puzzled by the notion of Atonement – I would sit at the feet of anyone who would try to explain the doctrine. Both matters baffled me. That is, until today. Today I learned how to act in relation to that laundry strike by getting deep into the meaning of the Atonement. It's incredible. I can hardly take it in.'

[* This approach is detailed and explained in an appendix of my book *Reinventing Theology as the Peoples' Work* (Wild Goose Publications).]

REFLECTION

Theology is the faith-basis for changing history in the direction of the Kingdom of God (ie the whole fabric of life structured God's way).

PRAYER

Lord God,

You are God most high. We have no means of knowing you other than that which you choose to provide. It is of your grace that you have disclosed to us your mind and purpose. Such knowledge is too wonderful for us: it is too high for us to attain. We humble ourselves before your loving concern for us.

We offer such a frail understanding in response; misreading your will, misinterpreting your purposes. So often we fail to glimpse the mystery of your being because of its range and depth and quality. So often we fail wilfully, ill-at-ease with love's demand and promise which asks so much of us, forgetting what it cost you.

If only we could separate thought and deed we would offer you the worship of our thoughts. But true worship involves the offering up of our whole beings, nothing held back. You are set on the transformation of this earth in justice, truth and peace: if we would know you we must join you in that struggle, as partners. We confess a reluctance to take that risk.

Lord God,

We thank you that you torment us by calling us to your service, by letting us know what you are about, by inviting us to share with you in your mission of transformation, by providing theology as the springboard for action.

Enable us to respond, rejoicing.

We ask it in Jesus Christ's name. Amen.

INDUSTRIAL DISCOVERIES

IN Selly Oak Colleges the mornings of one whole week were laid aside so that mission students and industrial students might together examine proposals for products not connected with the arms trade, put forward by Lucas Aerospace shop-floor workers. We hired a BBC film on the subject and showed it from time to time during the week. I was mandated to invite both the management and the trade unions of the firm to take part. They asked me to meet with them.

I found that, although the proposals had been made known to the public for several years, it took that outside initiative to bring management and trade unions round one table to speak together about them. At the end of some hours' discussion both agreed to be represented and did so with a fair measure of enthusiasm.

For students the gathering provided valuable insights into the way in which Christian faith and decisions in the world interact with one another. For Lucas Aerospace representatives it proved to be a time of new discoveries. We drew on biblical material to examine work and its meaning in life, to search for a true basis for relationships between masters and servants, to consider stewardship of the earth and its resources, to reflect on war and peace. They were astonished to find how relevant biblical texts were to the issues with which they were struggling in industry.

I was left with some questions.

Why should the general manager of Lucas Aerospace, a church member, find no initiative taken by fellow Christians to come alongside and seek to understand the complicated decisions he had to make, so that by prayer and support they might share his burden?

Why should the convener of the Combine Committee, an atheist and Marxist, never have previously encountered biblical faith where it could be seen to be relevant to the concrete realities of life in the industrial world?

Where are we Christians when we are needed?

PRAYER

*Father, Son and Holy Spirit, your loving care for the world extends
to all the processes by which we bring life forward and all the
organisations and institutions by which it is daily sustained.*

 – *Holy Father, when you created the sky, sea and land in all their
glory and with all their hidden treasures, you made the earth
rich and fertile and set us to tend and keep it. You blessed the
work of our hands. It was by our industry that earth yielded its
fruits, by the invention of machines and the harnessing of
power that these were produced on a scale to satisfy human
need. The way we handle the earth and develop machines and
value human labour are all matters for your fatherly care.*

  • *so let us be your children, acting responsibly with regard to
the earth's development.*

 – *Jesus Christ, the Son, you know what it was to work with your
hands. You also knew the mysteries of growth, of seedtime and
harvest. You knew what it was like to be in an occupied country
with a military machine ever ready to crush opposition. You
knew of swords and ploughshares; and the promise that one
would be turned into the other. In it all you were at work
redeemingly, offering new hope to people trapped in systems.*

  • *so let us be your brothers and sisters, acting responsibly to
free people from despair.*

 – *Holy Spirit of God, you give us visions of a better life, of a
society turned from warlike to constructive pursuits. You give us
a spirit of hope, encouraging us to press on against difficulties.
You nerve our spirits for the struggles to change the world in
the direction of the Kingdom. In all this you do not overbear
our spirits but plead with them, cajole them, love them into
longings for a better world.*

  • *so let us be kindred spirits, acting responsibly to spread the
flame of your love.*

We ask it in the name of Jesus Christ. Amen.

MUNICH (1972)

THE World Council of Churches mandated me to act as a chaplain at the Munich Olympics. Before committing myself I felt that I had to make sure that the assignment would not be an intrusion on the precious time and space needed by athletes. Chris Brasher and I talked this out over a meal. He appreciated my hesitations, but said there was a real job to be done if it were approached sensitively. The way to go about it was to make as natural a contact as possible with teams, and leave any further developments to the initiative of the members.

The British were well provided for with chaplains, so I moved to Commonwealth teams. Usually I would find a team gathered round a television, assessing form on the track. When an event finished they would exchange tips relevant to their own events. In time they would notice me. When I introduced myself, they unfailingly invited me to join them. African teams were especially welcoming.

It was the Olympics of dark memories. One day I stood outside a building where Palestinians held Jewish athletes hostage. Then came the shoot-out. As a result, the Games were abandoned for one day.

That day the mood had changed dramatically. The business of winning or losing was thrust into the background. Questions of life and death had become preoccupying. Athletes who had been in full health a day or two ago had been robbed of life. Some of them were known personally. What was life for? How does the fact of our dying, and not knowing how or where, affect the way we should live?

They did not look to me for answers. They included me in their search for meaning.

REFLECTION

Deep in human beings who seem to be preoccupied otherwise, is a questioning about the purpose of life. A serious accident, a partner walking out on a marriage, a terrorist bomb, a fall from a roof, an international incident – any such thing can trigger a questioning about the essentials by which we should live.

Deep in the human psyche lies the weight of wrongs done in past history and never put right, perhaps never tackled, perhaps not even given serious attention. At some point, these can result in an explosion which might seem out of proportion, even out of character. We need to ask not just about appearances of things but about what has been festering underneath the surface.

PRAYER

Holy Spirit of God, you work in the secret recesses of life, in the secret recesses of human hearts:
Work, we pray, in the recesses of our hearts to make us responsive to you in dealing with situations.
So that, when there is a word to say, we say it
when silence is needed we offer it
when companionship is what matters,
we are found alongside others,
not distant from them.
Holy Spirit of God, when we try to cover over past unrepented mis-deeds as if we could bury them and be free, remind us that they are alive and cry night and day for remedy, like Abel's blood.

When we accept the benefits which history has provided and live on the gains extracted by forebears by force, make us also conscious of our responsibility in present history: so that we take the side of those who would see that injustice is remedied and who build towards a true, just, peaceful society.
We ask it in Jesus Christ's name. Amen.

THE MENACING SHADOW

BEFORE my father lost his sight completely, when my brother and I were still too young to rise early to help him with his work, he made his way to our butcher's shop himself, at times falling over ashbuckets in Tolbooth Street on the way.

In summer the front door of the shop would be replaced by a wire door which let in cool air to freshen the shop overnight. On one occasion, when removing it, he became aware of a living and silent mass over against the entrance to the shop. Nothing in his previous experience indicated what it might be. He crossed the pavement, stretched out his arm – and put his hand on an elephant in Forres High Street! A circus had arrived in town. Its keeper had taken out the beast for an early stroll and had stabled it there while he went down the close for a bucket of water to give it a drink.

There was some menacing mass, equally undefinable, which I was aware of as I grew up in that area. It camped on the doorstep of my mind and would not go away. Only in my early twenties did I realise what it was – the Clearances. People had been cleared off the land, their homes burned over their heads to provide empty space for the pasturing of sheep, and later, deer. The grief of the extruded people was compounded by the attitude of so many clergy who attributed the calamity to the sins of the people when it should have been attributed to the greed and ruthlessness of the landlords.

Morayshire had itself felt the consequences. A fishing industry was established in the Moray Firth, at cost. Lives and boats had been lost through inexperience. People expelled from their highland farms broke their backs making rough, stony land fertile, only to have rents raised so that they had to move on and allow others to reap the benefit.

When past history, unredeemed, no longer lodges in the mind, it stays menacingly in the blood.

PRAYER

God the Lord,

*Only in the life of Jesus Christ can we see signs of what it must
have cost you to go on trusting us throughout our history. His suffering absorbed into the divine life the pains, the frustrations, the
disappointments, the agony, the dereliction which would otherwise
have gone on festering age after age, suppurating, erupting,
endlessly menacing the search for peace with justice.*

*We give you praise and glory that, in addition to what you
endured in the long centuries before Jesus Christ's coming, you made
him the Scapegoat to accept the burden of the whole world's sin and
bear it away. He made himself sin who knew no sin, that we might be
freed from sin.*

Yet we have to 'make up his sufferings' in the time committed to us.

*Help us, we pray, in his name and strength to take on ourselves
wrongs never righted committed by our nation on others, committed
within our nation by the strong on the weak.*

- *Forbid that nations should be enslaved by debts incurred by
  powerful interests and wily negotiators, which crush the poor
  decade after decade.*
- *Forbid that moneylenders should control the lives of those
  who have little to live on, so that they can never escape.*
- *Forbid that the destruction of precious cultures by overdomi-
  nating world trends should go unrecognised, unrepented.*
- *Forbid that the sexual and economic exploitation of the weak
  go unchallenged.*
- *Forbid that the wretched of the earth believe you to be absent,
  remote from their sufferings.*

Lord God,

*Here I am in history inheriting many advantages from past history.
When I say 'forbid', I also say 'here am I: send me'. Amen.*

FREEDOM AND DISCIPLINE

FOR five years, while carrying out the work of Rosyth parish, I was also 'in the Labour interest' Convener of Streets and Lighting in Dunfermline Town Council, whose boundaries included Rosyth. When it was time to leave after twelve years in the parish, the Conservatives sent a message through one of their number, Mr Kyle an elder, conveying good wishes and expressing appreciation of my explicit political commitment, which had spurred them to more vigorous engagement in their own cause; and of my policy of not using the pulpit for making *party* political points.

As an Independent, I would have been more cleanhanded and less relevant. Council decisions are built up on majorities. At pre-Council meetings every member is free to express any view at all about agenda points. When it comes to the Council itself majority decisions are meant normally to be supported. An overall set of priorities, on the basis of which any councillor was elected, could be threatened if everyone at that stage spoke and voted just as it came up their back.

Only on one occasion did I speak and vote against a judgment commonly reached. I was carpeted. It was one of the most frightening experiences I have ever endured. It was as if my liver had been taken out, chewed into little pieces, and replaced. If ever there was an encounter which made you feel 'I am a worm and no man', that was it.

Yet it was right that I should have voted as I did. It is right that the party should have acted as it did. Freedom and discipline belong together.

REFLECTION

Is not Jethro a biblical hero? Coming from outside the tradition of the chosen people, he brought to it fresh eyes and fresh ideas. He advised that personal judgment be replaced by institutional provision when the weight of responsibility became too much for one person to bear. Subsidiary courts would be likely to do better for both accusers and accused than would a tired Moses! ~ See Exodus 18 ~

PRAYER

Lord God,
We give thanks for political institutions which are sensitive to the needs and will of the people: so that, where majorities are heeded and minorities protected, we can achieve a reasonable way of managing life
  — and we acknowledge that not more than a reasonable way of managing life is open to us. We are human and fallible as are the institutions which we establish.
We give thanks for law courts and for legal aid giving access to justice to those who otherwise could not afford it.
We give thanks for those trained in the law, instructed in its intricacies, who act as advocates, prosecutors, judges of cases.
  — and we give thanks that ordinary people with no such skills can still be heard, the points they make weighed and judiciously assessed.

Save us, we pray, from living in imagined worlds where ideal solutions exist.
Grant us, we pray, acceptance of the world-as-is, grateful for it even with its imperfections, and grateful for the strong provision for sustaining the good life which its best institutions supply.
    In Jesus Christ's name. Amen

'OUT OF THE MOUTH ....'

WHAT was it like to be the child of a Christian home growing up under a Communist regime in which Christian faith was treated as an irrelevance and a delusion? In Brno, in 1991, Pastor Gerhard Linn of the World Council of Churches shared with me his own family's experience.

As the child of a pastor in the DDR, his son had been mocked, made the butt of jokes, marginalised and hounded – until he lost all interest in schooling and was badly traumatised. The teacher who encouraged the class to make sport of him did this so skillfully that Gerhard could not obtain firm evidence to challenge her behaviour.

When daughter Vera was ready for school, Gerhard and his wife postponed her starting time till she was seven years old in order to prepare her better for what she would be up against. Her parents would have sent her to religious instruction provided by the congregation on church premises. But she asked that this too be postponed. She said that she needed time to know her school classmates first. When she did turn up it was with five of these who, to the chagrin of the school teacher, had been helped by her to see the significance of Christian faith.

A boy mocked her, saying: 'You believe in God? Show me where you can see him!' She put him down firmly: 'Stupid ass! How can any-one or anything possibly be God that you can see!'

At about the age of ten or eleven, a class committee had to be appointed. The teacher told the pupils that a chairman would need to be chosen. She had, up her sleeve, the name of an ideologically acceptable pupil. But before she could get the name out, the whole class shouted 'Vera!' Their verdict had to be accepted.

The following year the teacher took Vera aside and told her how awkward it would be if she were to stand again for office. Vera agreed not to do so. 'You see, dad,' she explained, 'it doesn't matter who is officially appointed: it's me they'll turn to in any case.'

REFLECTION

You Shall Be Witnesses
I will pour out my spirit on all flesh
your sons and daughters shall prophesy
your old men shall dream dreams
and your young men shall see visions.
Even on the male and female slaves
in those days I will pour out my spirit.
~ Joel 2: 28, 29 ~

PRAYER

God of infinite mercy and lovingkindness,
We pray for those living under regimes, secular or religious, to
whose beliefs they do not subscribe, who are made the butt of jokes
and harassment: may they be given the courage and quick wit to get
the better of their tormentors, and not be damaged or traumatised to
their long-term hurt
— and we pray for those who are bullied at school, set on at
every turn, made to feel odd and wretched, that children's
rights may be effectively enforced.
We give you thanks that you have chosen young people, seemingly
weak, to tell forth your glory: that out of their lips you have perfected
praise
— and we pray for those who take bold action to share their faith
and hope with friends, in circumstances which make it a hard
thing to do: may the prayers of the whole church sustain and
hearten them.
We ask forgiveness for what we allow to happen in public life and
in playgrounds: and pledge ourselves to root out, as far as may be in
our power, practices which demean and devalue others in our society.
Lord, hear our prayer
and let our cry come to you. Amen.

DOORS OF HOPE

CATHEDRAL doors, over the centuries, have provided opportunities for skilled woodworkers to interpret the great moments of salvation history in carved figures, so that the learned and unlearned might be instructed.

Yet none that I have seen can match the doors of Oscar Romero's cathedral in San Salvador.

Traditional doors may have once stood there. The hostility to Romero and what he stood for could well mean that the original doors had been disfigured by being hacked or burned. What I do know is that the doors which I saw, shortly after the Archbishop's murder, provided an image which will stick in my mind forever.

They were made of plain planks of wood. Instruction in what pertained to the kingdom of God had been registered not with hammer and chisel, but with aerosols. Here again the learned and unlearned could understand. Every available space was covered by the cries of the people:

'End the Oppression' ... 'Down with the Junta' ...
'Justice or Death' ... 'Our Hope is in God' ...
'God is the Judge not the Junta.'

REFLECTION

'Rouse yourself! Why do you sleep O Lord?
Awake, do not cast us off forever.
Why do you hide your face?
Why do you forget our affliction and oppression?
For we sink down to the dust,
our bodies cling to the ground.
Rise up, come to our help.
Redeem us for the sake of your steadfast love.'
~ Psalm 44: 23-26 ~

Moses, told that God had heard the cries of the people in Egypt because of their taskmasters and had come down to deliver them, was deputed: 'I will send you to Pharaoh.' Today God hears cries, prepares deliverance and sends us.

Oscar Romero was already with his people, but still was sent to them. He was conservative by natural inclination; but the sheer pressure of the oppression led him to confront the military and become a martyr. Conservative and radical alike are called to confront injustice in God's name and ride the storm which follows, with God's power.

- *Strongmen who oppress their people are often armed by Western countries. Responsibility for instruments of oppression lies not far from our door:*
- *pray that the arms industry be curtailed and contained;*
- *pray that governments who will lose income may find alternative creative civilian forms of production in which to invest;*
- *pray that those who would lose work may be helped to find non-military alternatives.*
  - *Try to share the pain, grief and anger of oppressed people all over the world. Imagine, as vividly as possible, what it is like to have family and friends imprisoned, tortured, killed; what it is like to awake each day not knowing whether it may be your turn to be imprisoned, tortured, killed.*

Pray Lord God, if I am tested severely, let me be found faithful. Amen

2

IN GOD'S CHURCH

Renewing Church
Church alive
Basic christian communities
Biblical resources

FREED FOR GOD

BISHOP Labayan confided to me that when he was made bishop of his diocese in the north of the Philippines, he did not know how to set about the job. So in 1973 he summoned a Pastoral Congress, inviting representatives from every part of the diocese to attend so that he could listen to them and speak with them. They had been accustomed to follow a lead from the hierarchy. They found it difficult to take responsibility for thinking their own thoughts and sharing them with the new bishop. At the end of the conference, moved by some intuition of the Spirit, he gave them a final message: 'I free you to find what the Word of God is saying to you today.'

At first nothing happened. It went on happening. But, in time, members' curiosity led them to look with fresh eyes on life as they experienced it and then at life as God wanted it to be. They noted the contrast, asked themselves how this comes about – and went on to identify problems which needed to be confronted. They considered how they could claim the power of Jesus Christ to put their situation to rights, searching the scriptures for guidance.

By this time, they were forming small groups to get further into these matters. Nuns took part, adding quality by non-dominating participation. These basic christian communities provided a way of being a church which gave the whole business of living the faith a more local, personal focus. People took a fresh interest in the bible and found in it power to combat injustice right where they were. They became mature, active as never before.

To find what the word of God was saying to people in their time proved to be a lifegiving challenge. A few sparks produced a forest fire.

REFLECTION AND PRAYER

– *Think sympathetically of people given new assignments who do not know how to cope with them: and how the very inability to cope may open up possibilities for exploring fresh approaches to living the Christian life.*

Holy Spirit of God, we bless you that yours is an unbeatable spirit and that those who turn to you and trust in you, uncertain what to do for the best, may yet help others to walk in new ways, inspired by your leading.

– *Think sympathetically of people invited to take responsibility for 'being church' which they had previously placed on the shoulders of the clergy.*

– *Think sympathetically of the change from security to risk demanded of them.*

Holy Spirit of God, you probe deeply into the minds of your beloved human family. You are aware of their fears and hesitations. Empower them to offer their gifts in worship and service. Give those who might hinder them the grace to step aside, that your will might be done.

– *Think sympathetically of those seeking to form christian communities when they do not know how to go about it; of wrong directions which might be taken and the frustration and depression which may be engendered. May all be alert to the possibility that the closing of some doors may lead to the opening of others.*

Holy Spirit of God, you not only guide and inspire, but leave us free to make mistakes; then you encourage us not to give up but to learn from our failures. Help us with your support to press on without being discouraged, living by the light we see and ever looking for new light.

– *Think sympathetically of people in apathetic times – when committed people seem to be getting nowhere and nothing creative is happening.*

Holy Spirit of God, help us to wait on you as well as work with you so that we are patient in barren times and do not try to force your hand.

We ask it in the name of Jesus Christ. Amen.

GENUINE AUTHORITY

CAN hierarchies be made flexible and dynamic? Bishop Escaler of Ipil diocese in Mindanao showed Margaret and myself that they could, when we visited in 1982. The secret was: take a pyramidical structure and make a spiral of it; then press the spiral down – it becomes a spring !

In that diocese, 1200 basic christian communities met each week to find biblical resources for living the faith in local situations. Their discoveries, questions, testimonies, prayers were drawn into a *capilya* (chapel) service on Sundays. Every month there was a *zona* gathering, lasting two days, when the leaders, whom the members themselves had chosen, (a) got further training in handling the scriptures and (b) also challenged one another if it was thought that forms of leadership were becoming manipulative. *Parishes* covered a wider area. *Districts* each covered one-third of the diocese. Finally a *Prelature Assembly* of 150 people took an overview of developments in the whole diocese. Four times a year the spring gathered dynamic from the basic christian communities and tightened its coils into the *Prelature Assembly*; then unwound to nourish the christian community all the way back to the grass roots.

On the steering committee of the Assembly priests and nuns were in the minority. Bishop Escaler did not even chair the gathering. That was left to a layman. The bishop took a seat among the other representatives in the main body of the hall.

Bishop Escaler just *had* authority. He did not need to pull rank, as with those whose authority is shaky. His authority was like Jesus', unforced. You can give away that kind of authority and still have it.

PRAYER

Lord God Almighty,
look on us with mercy who are at one and the same time constricted
and disabled by the institutional church, and grateful for its gifts.

We strain against the yoke
when the Holy Spirit directs us in new ways and the institution
holds us back, fearful of losing power, fearful of that venturing which
might undermine its certainties, protective of its authoritarian position;
we pray for those seeking new ways of being church, especially in
basic christian communities – wherever the traditional church seeks
to suppress the new life instead of fostering it; and for all ventures in
faith.

We strain against the yoke
yet it is the yoke which bends us to necessary tasks, makes these
fruitful to produce a harvest, provides resources of stored grain
against winter storms;
we pray for those who undertake thankless and boring assign-
ments to sustain the institution – attending to buildings, administration
and finance; for those who organise means for meeting and mission;
for those in authority who, for the good of the whole church, are
protective of orthodox beliefs and life;
for authorities who keep in touch both with higher ecclesiastical
authorities and with what is bursting from below through the Spirit,
hoping to reconcile what appears to be irreconcilable. We ask your
grace for those in authority who take the lead in pioneering new ways.

Grant, we pray, that 'movement' and 'institution' may so honour
you that, together, they enable the church to build itself up in love.
Amen.

PRAISE GOD WITH TAMBOURINES AND DANCING*

WHEN I served on Dunfermline Town Council during the 1950s, councillors became concerned about the crowds of young people who roamed the streets of a Sunday evening with nothing to do except get up to mischief. I publicly supported those who favoured the opening of dance halls. My advocacy was reported in the national newspapers. That upset my mother: 'We are asked to keep only one day of the week for God!'

'No, seven,' I replied.

It took a long time for that hurt to heal.

On Iona, on one occasion, a lass skilled in helping people to express the faith in dance wanted to make a team contribution during worship which I was conducting. I looked at what she suggested. It would have been extraneous to the service. So I turned down that request. But instead of having a stand-off we got our heads together and worked out an alternative. Those who took part in the worship agreed that the dance drama which resulted provided an imaginative exposition of the scriptural theme, adding a dimension which words could not convey.

When the time came to move from Scottish Churches House, Dunblane to Geneva, we were farewelled at a service in Dunblane Cathedral. The occasion was planned to be one of rejoicing. It had been possible to establish a House of the Churches Together as a base for their common life and outreach in Scotland. We would express this in prayer, testimony, praise.

In anything else?

The service ended with Sydney Carter's hymn, 'Lord of the Dance'. A dancing congregation moved out into the cathedral square where an open-air dance rounded off the celebration.

[*From Psalm 150: 4.]

REFLECTION

Sing to the Lord a new song
his praise in the assembly of the faithful ...
Let them praise his name with dancing ...
For the Lord takes pleasure in his people ...
~ Psalm 149: 1, 3, 4 ~

Our bodies are temples of the Holy Spirit: and she is a dancing Spirit.
Dancing can be associated with excess – drugs, sexual irrespon-
sibility. Its rejection can also be associated with excess – respectability,
self-righteousness, prejudice.
Our bodies should witness to where our lives are rooted. Is it not
a betrayal of our bodily existence to over-indulge them or debase
them? Then is it not also a betrayal to treat them like a musical
instrument which is locked in its case and laid aside – as if owner-
ship were enough without music-making?

PRAYER

We pray for shy people who find bodily expression awkward,
that, as time goes on, they may feel more and more at home in
their bodies.
We pray for people who fail to honour their bodies,
making them available carelessly for superficial relationships
or evil pursuits.
We pray for those driven by poverty to sell their bodies in order to
survive, whether by prostitution or by sweat-shop labour.
We pray for those abused in childhood whose bodies have become
blemished strangers.
We give thanks for the Martha Grahams of this world
who have opened up new ways of expression in dance.
May the whole world celebrate that second exodus
which was accomplished in Jerusalem by Jesus Christ.
We ask it in the name of the Lord of the Dance. Amen.

REDISCOVERING THE ESSENCE

IN the early 1970s some Roman Catholic basic christian communities in Holland felt that they had to identify the essence of Christian living, separate that out from non-essentials and concentrate on implementing a way of life which expressed it.

They looked at the bible. 'The priest's book,' they concluded, 'selected and interpreted in ways which suit his purposes and secure his control over the people. Out of the window with it!'

They looked at the Mass. 'A rigmarole,' they concluded, 'designed to perpetuate priestly domination. It does not help the church to become adult in faith. Out of the window with it!'

In what then lay the essential core of the gospel? 'The establishment of justice on earth,' they concluded. 'We will concentrate on answering that challenge.'

Before long they came round full circle: 'We don't know what justice is without the bible; we are not nourished for the struggles without the sacrament.'

They showed a double maturity in abandoning church practices which held no meaning for them and in still keeping an eye on these in case there was more in them than they had previously recognised.

Was it worthwhile going out only to come back to where they had started? The joy they exhibited in renewed sacramental worship, the excitement in searching the scriptures would never have been theirs had they not been willing to leave behind what was meaningless, and also been willing to reassess its quality and centrality in the light of experience.

REFLECTION

*As a prelude to announcing Jesus Christ to the Areopagus gathering
of philosophers in Athens, Paul looked for general human territory
on which to take his stand.*

~ Acts 17: 22-31 ~

*All human beings have it in them 'to seek God in the hope that,
groping after him they might find him,' he said, and quoted their own
poets, who called human beings 'God's offspring'.*

*In this Age of Faith, of exploration and questioning (to be distin-
guished from an Age of Certainty), are there not many who experience
that restlessness, within the Christian tradition; who search on the
fringes of the church, not because the church asks too much of them
but because it asks too little; who reckon that there is more to the faith
than the official church affirms? It may well be from the fringes of the
traditional church that new insight and venturing come to renew its life.*

PRAYER

Then pray:

*For all those who are willing to leave safe ground and go
searching, prepared for discoveries of faith's demand and promise
which will turn their lives upside down and test them to the full: who
can provide a goodly heritage for generations which follow.*

*For communities in their quest for ways of being church which
are more adventurous and imaginative than those which they had
inherited – these to be contributed as a gift for the renewal of the
whole church.*

*For those who have affirmed the traditional faith through hard
and testing times and held to its essentials till these were reappreciated
and reappropriated.*

*... and examine yourself to see whether you too lightly and
unquestioningly accept the tradition in which you were brought up,
or too lightly and unthinkingly are ready to discard it.*

A CALLING DISCOVERED

TO be an elder in Rosyth Parish Church in the 1950s was a demanding and rewarding task.

The responsibility of elders was not only to care for their portion of the flock. It was also to see that members were caring for their neighbours, extending to others around the friendship with which they had been embraced in the church family. People would hesitate to accept nomination to fill vacancies in the kirk session, for it was not an honorary or formal position but a committing one.

On one occasion when potential elders had been nominated by the congregation, I met with them for a whole evening. We examined what eldership had been in New Testament times and in our own Reformed tradition. Several doubts and difficulties were dealt with. But one or two felt that they did not have the spiritual resources required to tackle the job (and did not see that such diffidence is a qualification, not a disqualification!). We agreed to leave them to mull over the options and to meet again a week later.

When we did come together as agreed I found that they had already met for two evenings in the intervening time, one of their number leading in prayer, each speaking of the biblical role as he* understood it, seeking together to discover their calling.

Now all were humbly prepared to go forward.

[*Since that time, women have also become eligible.]

REFLECTION

Christ is like a single body with its many limbs and organs
which, many as they are, together make up one body ...
Now you are Christ's body and each of you a limb or organ of it.

~ 1 Corinthians 12: 12, 27 ~

PRAYER

God the Lord,
You have not only made us for yourself. You have made us with
such various qualities, accomplishments, skills, talents that, combined,
they may tell out the myriad glories of your being;
You have not only made us for yourself. You have equipped us
with strength, courage, tenacity to work with you for the transfor-
mation of this world. The different status accorded to us in the world's
eyes has no weight with you for whom there are first that shall be last
and last that shall be first.
You furnish your church with ministries which enrich its
worship and enlarge its service in the world.

Today we pray for the ministry of elders:
– remembering the pressure upon their time, the need to do justice
  to family, work and church responsibilities and still find space to
  be themselves;
– remembering feelings of inadequacy they may harbour;
– remembering the gifts which, well deployed, may help others to
  mature in faith and life.
We ask you to give them new heart should their spirit fail at times:
  that they may be like leaven in the lump of the world's apathy
  to change stodgy material into wholesome bread.

We ask it in Jesus Christ's name. Amen.

A REAL TEAM

IN 1940 I was a student leader of the 'Challenge of the Faith' Week, a mission to Edinburgh University. We had 'heavy guns' to call on — George MacLeod and Mervyn Stockwood. For a team of three, one member remained to be chosen, a lady missioner. The lot fell on Isobel Forrester, wife of Professor Forrester of St Andrews. She was apprehensive at first at the prospect. She had been rearing a family, looking after the good of students — but never anticipating playing so public a role. Hers was a genuine reluctance. In the end, with some trepidation, she consented.

George and Mervyn were powerful orators, giving the message with convincing authority. A third orator would have 'sunk the ship by the weight of its guns'.

But Isobel Forrester went quietly among the students, listening, sharing her own experience and insights, doing so ever so gently so that they were prepared to travel in their thinking with her. Her grace and charm were a testimony in themselves to the faith she held. Margaret, later to be my wife, at that point not a convinced Christian, found that Isobel's approach provided the space she needed to think through life's priorities in her own way and at her own pace. Others were similarly helped.

The great gift of the inexperienced is not to know, sometimes, what to do and what to say; or to speak with such modesty and reserve that the Holy Spirit is given room to work her work. The different giftedness of the three made them a real team.

PRAYER

Holy Spirit of God,
You see the possibilities in human beings which often they do not
see themselves; and when they respond you draw these out and mature
them to your praise and glory.
We bless your holy name.
You do not judge as we do, but affirm those who are willing to take
hesitant steps in strange territory. You cover their frail faith with your
large provision.
We bless your holy name.
If you send us to a task and we are unfit for it, you create, from
nowhere, qualities which have been lacking; so that we find our-
selves adequately equipped for the service you ask of us.
We bless your holy name.
If we are in the company of spiritual giants, you make that a
special favour instead of a disheartening put-down. You do not see
as we see. You enable us to rejoice at the greatness of others and not
be disheartened. Your grace is sufficient for us, your strength made
perfect in weakness.
We bless your holy name.

So take us as we are, Spirit of God, use us as you will,
for your touch has the power to revive drooping spirits
and to make all things possible to those who believe.

Let us not take our own estimate of ourselves as a measure of fitness
for tasks, but rely on your willingness to supply every need:
that we may testify to you among the nations
and turn many to the true Way of Life.

We ask it for your own name's sake. Amen.

WHAT IS MISSION

WHEN Billy Graham's first visit to Britain was on the cards, the British Council of Churches was asked to make a declaration of support for his mission. In Scotland, lay people had been enabled to develop gifts and take a new decisive place in church life through the 'Tell Scotland' movement and 'Kirk Weeks'. In addition they had the inspiration of the Iona Community and the new resource of Scottish Churches House. I was concerned, with justification as it turned out, that massive assemblies, where the speaking would be all from the front, would cut the cord of lay initiatives, though ostensibly they were designed to encourage these. For me Ephesians 4 was decisive, with its picture of the church being built up from below by the whole membership.

At the consultative meeting in our region I spoke strongly against the venture. In the British Council of Churches' debate I argued passionately and successfully against a request for the Council's support, adding my concern about Billy Graham's close ties with the US President Nixon, and his failure to raise any protest about the secret war in Cambodia. Dictators such as President Park of Korea proved to be only too delighted to roll out the red carpet for such missions. They offered no challenge to dictatorships' exploitation and suppression of the people.

Was I right or wrong? I have met many people for whom the mission was a turning point in life. So should we say that every form of evangelism should be given its chance?

I still believe that the pouring of energy of the 'Tell Scotland' Movement into this mission distracted from and hindered the development of the whole people of God in Scotland.

PRAYER

God of all grace,
You have set before us a way of life and a way of death, yet which is which is often not clear, though we must choose. Save us from offending others unnecessarily through thoughtless action or needless hurt. Yet make us prepared to see others take offence if truth is genuinely at stake.

You see as we do not, and our grasp on truth is frail and uncertain. So take not your Holy Spirit from us
> *who sees the whole context in which choices have to be made;*
> *who understands the thoughts of our hearts, both in their*
>> *deceitfulness and in their longing to exhibit integrity in life and action;*
> *who can bring glory out of moral grime;*
> *who is sufficient for all our weaknesses.*

We pray for mass evangelists; especially when they are tempted to exclude tough talk, especially to principalities and powers.
We pray for ordinary people who are prepared to become adults in understanding and to exercise a full ministry: that they may have time and opportunity to make growth in faith without being fitted into moulds prepared by others.

Lord,
> *that there may be a harvest, bless the seed which grows secretly.*
> *We ask it in Jesus Christ's name. Amen.*

NO DISTANT GOD

ALBERT Einstein, reflecting on the rise of Naziism in Germany, spoke of how he had looked to universities, thinkers, writers and editors to defend freedoms, and had looked in vain. He went on: 'I never had any special interest in the church before, but now I feel a great affection and admiration because the church alone had the courage and persistence to stand up for intellectual truth and moral freedom.'

That takes ingenuity as well as courage.

I found this when, in 1995, I revisited Wilgespruit Fellowship Centre near Johannesburg after an absence of a quarter of a century. In 1970 with apartheid at its height, the Centre had insisted on providing space for multi-racial gatherings. I found that the God of Abraham, Isaac and Jacob had been at work all through the years between.

There had been an Abrahamic determination to leave behind the laager of apartheid and seek a city which had foundations, whose builder and maker is God.

There had been persistence in the face of severe setbacks, akin to those of Isaac who, when wells he dug were taken over, dug more until opponents gave up.

Imaginative action to outwit authorities had resembled that of Jacob, the Godly Twister. When it was decreed that no more than 72 hours, later reduced to 48, could be spent at the Centre by any one group, people were bussed to a neighbouring municipality, photographed there and brought back to the centre as a fresh contingent. When the Christian Institute was banned and it looked as if Wilgespruit would follow suit, a judge was found, ex-Rhodesian, who had defied UDI and resigned. He agreed to head an ecclesiastical commission, which refuted the findings of the official enquiry into the Centre's doings.

An African woman testified to me approvingly: 'No family in South Africa is blacker than the Whytes.'

PRAYER

God of Abraham,

We are blessed by his faith and that of Sarah, when they went out not knowing where they would end up. We today profit from things discovered through their journeying with you, which would not have been revealed had they stayed at home.

We bless you for that venturing, and the venturing of those who followed: and pray that when the call comes to us, we may respond with like faith.

God of Isaac,

We rejoice in the gifts you can give even through beings who are traumatised, as Isaac was, who saw his father's knife poised above him ready to rob him of life.

We bless you for his non-combative nature, and his persistence in face of contending tribesmen so that, robbed of one well, he went on to dig another, till a whole valley was made fertile.

We bless you for his patience; and for the tenacity of those who follow in his steps: and pray that we may show a like resilience.

God of Jacob,

We rejoice in the gifts you provide to outwit authorities who seek their own advantage and deny people their rights.

We bless you for Jacob's lively perception, in situations he faced, of what was at stake; his quick-witted response to circumstances, his capacity to turn the tables on opponents. We give thanks for those who follow, using imaginative means to get the better of forces hostile to the gospel, its demands and promises.

We give thanks that there is not just one way of responding to you, God the Lord. Let us find the way which is right for us and for the people of our time. Amen

BUILT UP AS CHURCH

HOW would you have handled the following situation?

Adolescents and young adults lived in Poland in the 1970s under a Communist regime hostile to their faith. They were scattered about the country, restricted regarding travel, without physical means or finance to visit others of like conviction. How could they build one another up as church?

Halina Bortnowska, my contact for the World Council of Churches' 'Participation in Change' programme, was never short of imaginative ideas. She asked for two tape recorders, one to stay at base and the other to travel; and as many tapes as I could procure. A flow of ideas, insights, prayers, new and refreshing, began to circulate round Poland in the following way:

The first group might occupy about seven minutes of tape. They might reflect on the current situation from a Christian perspective; go on to quote a poem which had appealed to them; note an insight from scripture; offer a prayer and end with a hymn they had composed. Tape and tape recorder would be conveyed to the next group who would hear the previous group's contribution, make their own and, in turn, pass the recorder and tape to the next small community.

As a consequence of the Vatican II Council, Synods had to be set up. Unused as it was to such freedom, the Roman Catholic church in Poland did not know what to put on the agenda of these bodies. The young people, instructed by their taped conversations, were able to filter on to the agendas concerns which they thought important.

On just one occasion was it possible for me to meet with participants in this exercise – south of Krakow, close to the then Czechoslovak border.

How joyous was their faith!

And they were being built up in it by one another!

PRAYER

*Almighty and most **merciful** God,*
How you must have let your imagination run riot when you formed
the creation! How your eyes must have danced when you brought into
being a profusion of trees, plants and flowers, a profusion of creatures
adapted to land and sea, a profusion of birds of every kind. So many
different species, so many species different! All this against a living
back-cloth of sea, sky, mountain, river and plain!
May all that has breath glorify your name and praise you for
ever and ever.

*Almighty and most **gracious** God,*
What an imaginative leap was yours to make us caretakers of
your universe! For rocks and trees are dumb, animals birds sea-
creatures have limited speech. An articulate voice was needed. How
amazing was the scale of that thought which provided beings made
in you image, who know what it is to be at one with all that has breath
on the earth and yet can communicate with the Most High. So the
urging of creation towards its fulfilment, the urging of all things you
have made to give you glory can be caught up in human speech and
presented to you as a sacrifice of praise.
May we, the unworthy, justify your trust.

*Almighty and most **loving** God,*
How incredible the imagination which would take on board the
thought of the incarnation, your own coming-to-be-with-us!
You saw us failing in the responsibility entrusted to us. You could
have left it at that, unhitched our planet and let it spin useless
through a vacant universe. But your heart of love would not let us
go, would not let it go.
Holy holy holy God of power and might
heaven and earth are full of your glory.
Glory be to you O God Most High. Amen.

'HERE' MEETS 'THERE'

AT Selly Oak Colleges, Birmingham, Margaret had interests of her own to follow through. One was Tools for Self-Reliance. Tools lying around and rusting in sheds and garages could be gathered and refurbished by volunteers who had the skills and time. Complete chests, sufficient for the needs of a carpentry industry in a village or small town, could be provided for countries where such tools were of poor quality and were in short supply.

Margaret found retired people with necessary skills, and set up a once-a-week operation. One winter she and her team were given the use of the Cricket Pavilion at Selly Oak Colleges for the reconditioning work. It was there that the unexpected happened.

Two Tanzanians had been walking in the grounds nearby. Their path took them past the pavilion. They stuck their heads round the door, curious, and asked what was going on. When they were told they became animated.

They had seen the fruit of this project in their own country. A chest of tools had been delivered to a village. Up to that point carpenters had been struggling with inadequate, substandard equipment. Now a proper business could be established. People could put in orders for basic furniture confident that the project would deliver. Apprentices could be taken on. A timber industry could be promoted, and reafforestation started. Ancillary industries could develop on the side, generated by the increase of wealth and hope.

'The kind of thing you are doing *here*,' said the Tanzanians, 'can revitalise a whole area *there*.'

REFLECTION

'This *is* that,' *said St Peter at Pentecost.*
~ Acts 2: 16 ~

This *before your eyes is* that *which was prophesied by Joel in distant centuries, said Peter*
It takes imagination to connect distant things whose relationship to one another may be significant, yet may not at first spring to mind. Is not one of the great failures of our time the inability to connect what we do here (eg arms' exports) *with what is effected there* (violence and death); *what we do* here (*eg* Christian Aid) *with what is effected* there (new hope, new dignity)?
Television can bring home to us what is happening 'there'. But the 'here' requirement to meet that development or need can elude us, or its claim on us be deliberately suppressed.

PRAYER

Lord God,
You see all things and how they relate.

Prophets, looking deeply into the mystery of your being unmasked evil in their 'here and now'; and presaged a disastrous fruit, for those who rejected your ways, in years to come.
Forgive us that we are blind to the results of much of what we do
— especially where we choose to be blind, fending off awareness of consequences which would challenge our comfort.
Nourish our imagination that we may become sensitive to ways of life which are affected by decisions we make here and now.
Teach us your ways, O Lord, and lead us in right paths. Amen.

STANDING FOR THE RIGHT

IT was on a Sunday I landed in Korea. Ahn Jae-Woong was not at Seoul airport to greet me. There was no message in my room when I reached it. It was puzzling.

The next day I was up betimes and went to the nearby offices of the Korean Council of Churches. Ahn Jae-Woong's office was closed. I sought help in the General Secretary's Department. When they heard what I had come for, administrative staff became clearly ill at ease.

'I think he is out of the country,' hazarded one.

'He can't be,' I said. 'The workshop in which I am to share is due to start today. He had reserved the dates. They were clearly marked in his diary.'

'I think he is ill,' ventured another.

'Had he been ill,' I answered, 'he would have left a message at the airport or in my room. He is not the kind to leave someone hanging around without knowing where to go and what to do.'

The truth at last came in a whisper. 'He is in jail.'

The workshop in which I was to take part concerned action to establish a more just social order in that country. Ahn Jae-Woong, through his connection with the World Student Christian Federation and his concern for industrial mission, had set it up. The teaming up of industrial workers and students had been seen by the Park dictatorship as a threat to the status quo.

A red carpet would be rolled out to welcome prominent Christian evangelists. They posed no threat to the regime. They could be trusted to speak of justice and truth only in general terms. But Christian students and Christian industrial workers meeting to discern what God's order for Korea might be – in that lay a real threat to existing powers. Leaders of a peaceful demonstration leading up to the workshop had been jailed, Ahn Jae-Woong among them.

I reflected that, if it had been the first century and I had been visiting Peter or Paul, I might as likely have found them in jail.

REFLECTION

*The Lord works vindication
and justice for all who are oppressed.*
~ Psalm 103: 6 ~

*Say among the nations 'The Lord is King! ...
He will judge the peoples with equity.'*
~ Psalm 96: 10 ~

PRAYER

*We give you glory, honour and praise, Lord God, that you retain the
final judgment on all that happens on earth.*

*When people fight for justice for the oppressed and the oppressors
set out to crush them, you affirm their cause, intent on establishing a
world marked by justice, truth and peace.*

- *We give thanks for those who stand with you, and that you
  stand by them: for your will is not to transform the world
  by your strong right arm alone but to bring us to maturity
  by inviting us to work alongside you.*
- *We give thanks for those who are prepared to suffer, contending for the rights of the poor; not knowing what injury
  they will have to bear or what sentence will be imposed on
  them in consequence; gambling with their health, career,
  reputation to stand between the oppressed and the oppres-
  sor in Christ's name. May they have their reward; and see
  justice, truth and peace prevail.*
- *We confess that we flinch from standing for the right
      we ignore the summons to offer our bodies
          as a living sacrifice that right may prevail.
      Turn us and change us, good Lord,
          that your will for your beloved world
          may not be frustrated.
  We ask it in Jesus Christ's name. Amen.*

DISCOVERING AND UNDERSTANDING TRUTH

THE role of Dr George MacLeod in the Central Africa Federation struggles of the 1950s was commanding. He awoke Scotland to the possibility that a white-dominated racist bloc might be established, with Rhodesia as its model. His lead was followed widely. In Rosyth the Council of Churches could pack the Institute with over 200 people eager to hear representatives and leaders from that part of Africa. They provided information on features of the situation different from those given prominence in Parliament and in the media. The people of Rosyth became well instructed about what was at stake in Central Africa.

Strong ties bound the Church of Scotland to Nyasaland/Malawi. It was said that if you saw a circle of men debating under a tree you would not know whether it was a kirk session or a local Council meeting. The overlap between the two would at times be almost complete.

Officials at the Foreign Office pooh-poohed the churches' arguments, treated them as amateurish, lacking knowledge of significant facts. But their own attitude was marked by a readiness to find what they were looking for, an inclination to believe their own propaganda, a desire to find a line which superiors would approve. Such a mind-set can make official findings less reliable than those of people who simply do good homework on circumstances they seek to understand.

When the situation was resolved it was the churches, not the professionals, whose judgment was vindicated.

REFLECTION

*When the spirit of truth comes he will guide you
into all truth; for he will not speak on his own
but will speak whatever he hears, and he will declare
to you the things that are come.*

~ John 16: 13 ~

Accurate 'hearing' demands stringent disciplines. Research, statistical enquiry, testing of sources, analysis must accompany and check perceptions and reactions.

PRAYER

Lord God,
we human beings, commanded to replenish and subdue the earth, to stock and manage it, need to know both what stuff we are made of and what stuff we are called to handle
– so we pray for geographers, geologists, geochemists, geo-physicists, geomedicals, all geoscientists and environmental-ists who unlock the secrets of the earth, so that we may know what we are dealing with and give it the respect it is due.

Lord Christ,
when you redeemed the whole creation, which longs to see us living as children of God that it might find its own fulfilment, you committed us to live as responsible human beings, responsive to our neighbours, responsive to all living creatures, responsive to the needs of future generations, establishing justice
– so we pray for persons and organisations devoted to the freeing and fulfilling of those who are denied life;
for persons and organisations dedicated to combating racism.

Holy Spirit of God,
who brought people alive as never before at Pentecost, awaken our consciences so that we may take delight in finding the truth and doing it, to the honour and glory of your holy name. Amen.

SEEKING TRUTH

SERGIO Aquilante was later to become President of the Methodist Church in Italy. When we met him in 1973 he was pastor in San Sabastiano. The occasion was a consultation on church renewal.

The congregation had two distinctive features marking its life. It encouraged the invasion of land, underused or unused by large landowners; and helped landless peasants to secure it so that they could make it productive and feed their families. Since the values of the political establishment heavily impregnated the educational curriculum, the congregation ran a *doppo-scuela,* a school-after-school, in which children were alerted to underlying establishment assumptions impregnating education.

We sat in a horse-shoe shape in the church hall. Alongside Sergio was the Secretary of the local Communist Party of which Sergio was a card-carrying member.

Sergio led off with an appreciation of the tools which Marxism had provided for getting to grips with aspects of the malfunctioning of society. If we did not understand the dynamic forces at work and learn how to deal with them, we would all be their victims. We were destined to take charge of history, not to be its pawns. He then went on to say how totally inadequate Marxism was as a philosophy of life – a ridiculously superficial one compared with Christianity. It ignored the way in which sin penetrates all human life – including that of the proletariat and of elite vanguards; it lacked depth in addressing the pros and cons of nationalism: it held out no real hope for human life since achievements passed to heirs also died with them, and death had the last word.

We realised that he had two audiences in mind.

We were one.

He was also speaking right round the room to the invited guest beside him.

PRAYER

Lord Christ,
You said to your disciples, 'If you know these things, happy are
you if you do them'.
— We confess that we know and fail to do.
All over the world, land is unfairly distributed, taken by the power-
ful, denied to those who would tend it and feed their families.
We know that this is against your will.
We know that we are summoned to discover ways in which
power can be controlled for good but are held back because
we are afraid: of derision, of failure, of suffering.
So we bless you for Christian communities who dare and do,
and pray for our own conversion to the world you love
where you long to see justice abound.

— We confess that we know and fail to do.
When theories go out of fashion we are content to let them be
forgotten even when they have produced insights which have lasting
worth. We swim with the stream, content with large generalisations
and cheap condemnations. We know we should be alert to recognise
truth wherever it is to be found and fight for the truth, even when that
is unpopular. But we confess that we fall down.
You who are the Truth, help us to be more committed servants of
the truth lest the world lie in confusion, encouraged by our default.
We bless you for prophets of our time who sort out truth from
falsehood; and pray for our own conversion to a more prophetic life
so that, whatever the cost, we may be found at your side.
We ask it for your own name's sake. Amen

NEW LIFE

IN the early 1970s, through developing the World Council of Churches' 'Participation in Change' programme, I had been made aware of new life springing from the base of the church in Central America. Poor people were gaining confidence that they were made in the image of God, that God valued their life, that there was a place for them in God's purpose.

They came together in small groups around the bible and sought to find what God asked of them in order to deal faithfully with situations which faced them. Already in Medellin (1968) the description 'basic christian community' was given currency; but the people whom I contacted in Central America did not yet use that description.

However, I thought something fresh was brewing and invited representatives of those seeking new ways of living the Christian faith to meet. The spectrum of the invitation covered a figure 'C' starting in Puerto Rico and moving round to end up in Venezuela, where we assembled.

Our base was a Pentecostal Centre in Barquisimeto whose pastors lived at the same level as the poor campesinos whom they served. The accommodation was very basic. But that was just right for the kind of people who gathered. Had the conference been in a hotel, it would have taken them the whole five days to get over the culture shock! As it was, they established good communicating relationships with one another right away. They spoke different Spanish dialects, almost incomprehensible to me (it was as if Gaelic speakers from Ireland, Scotland and Wales conversed in seemingly different speech but could understand one another without problems).

One man upbraided me. He had been given his air ticket but not a penny more; and had arrived to find that the Centre was three miles from the airport. He had no money for transport or even for a phone call. 'But you have arrived' I responded. 'How did you get here?'

'I just went round the airport asking people, "Are you a Christian?" When I found a Christian with a car, I said, "You have to get me to the Pentecostal Centre". And he did!'

PRAYER

Father, Son and Holy Spirit,
> *we bless you who establish springs of life in unlikely places.*

Holy Father,
> *we bless you that, in our time, the poor and wretched of the earth
> have lifted up their heads, become aware of their high standing in
> your sight, looked up to you for life, thrown off the demeaning
> yoke of servitude and accepted Christ's light yoke in its place.
> This is a wonder and a joy to us. Glory to you, O Lord most High.*

Lord Christ,
> *who chose for your companions the lowliest and the least, look on
> us with mercy who have called the proud happy.
> You emptied yourself of reputation and status:
> May we learn afresh what true stature consists of from the 'little
> ones' of the earth.*

Holy Spirit of God,
> *who ceaselessly strives with the human spirit to give it new hope
> and teach it new ways,
> we have grown stale and cold, and need reviving with draughts
> from spiritual wells in other parts of the world.
> Forgive us, we pray, who are untouched so often by your work
> elsewhere,
> and grant us this grace:*
>> *that our eyes be opened to where you are at work
>> and our hearts be instructed to our own renewal
>> that we may have a share in the promised time
>> when the earth shall be filled with the knowledge of you
>> as the waters cover the sea. Amen.*

JAILED AT THE RIGHT TIME

'I WAS very fortunate,' said Father Juan Garcia Nieto. 'We were all fortunate. The secret police got wind of what I was doing and put me in jail. The timing was just right. Being in one of Franco's jails was no picnic. But in 1969 we had just formed a small Christian community. My removal meant that lay people had to shape that community without "benefit of clergy". They did so very imaginatively. They made a real church, a church born from below, a church not shaped by the straitjacket which those in power so often impose. They might otherwise have been depending on me too much. Once I was in prison, they had to get on with the job of being church, themselves.

'But is it not written: "I will smite the shepherd and the sheep shall be scattered?"'

'Yes, but the shepherd is not the ordained priest. It is Jesus Christ, and he remained with them. They took full responsibility to be church. When I was eventually released they already existed as a Christian community shaped in a priestless way. That made them more responsible for their life together. Different forms of leadership developed within the whole community. On my return I was simply accepted as one of their number, not someone over them.'

[From a reconstituted interview in Barcelona in 1980.]

'The existing community was born without a priest and that meant more debating and sharing. It was as people-who-knew-themselves-to-be-living-church that contact was made with the priest who later joined us. That relationship had elements of confrontation as well as debating and sharing. After all, we had been 6 years without a priest. We have celebrated the mass without a priest, though normally we go to the parish celebration.'

[En Quadraro basic christian community in Rome, 1983]

PRAYER

Lord Christ,
You provide for your church all that is needful.

In times of oppression, when the official leadership is removed, you raise up leaders from among those who would seem to have no gift for it; and remind us that God the Father, who out of stones can create children to Abraham, needs no authority other than his own to secure the fullness of the church;
which is your body, each part with its function contributing to the ministry of the whole.

In times of hardening arteries, where the known leadership of the church is almost paralysed, you raise up movements to give people fresh hope; and in and from these movements you raise up those whom you choose, making visible through them the many forms of leadership which are required to equip the church;
which is your body, each part with its function contributing to the ministry of the whole.

In times of change, where traditional forms are shaken, you raise up women and children to exercise significant ministries, and point the church to a fuller way of being church;
which is your body, each part with its function contributing to the ministry of the whole:

Till the time comes when you take the church to yourself
in splendour, without a spot or wrinkle or anything of the kind,
holy and without blemish. Hallelujah! Amen.

~ Ephesians 5: 27 ~

IT TAKES ALL SORTS

THE Machstrasse basic christian community in Vienna owed its origin to the perceptiveness of the priest who encouraged members of the congregation to develop their own initiatives and exercise a communal ministry alongside him. Parish worship and parish gatherings were too large to provide the depth of relationship which would allow the congregation to move forward. Small cells were put in place as well.

'How did you bring these into being?' I asked Trout, a member.

'First we learned a lesson the hard way,' she replied. 'We thought that, if such intimate communities are to work, they had better consist of people who get on with one another. So we identified people who were pretty like-minded and invited them to get together. Stuttering starts were made. Before long the whole enterprise collapsed. We had to go back to square one.

'I see it now as a sign of God's grace that the collapse took place. The basis on which we had proceeded was that of mutual compatibility. But that cannot be the foundation of Christian community. We do not choose one another. Community is created when we are chosen by God and given to one another. Often people who are not at all like-minded are chosen. But God gives them the grace to make community, which is enriched and strengthened by differences.

'We started again. This time we kept our eyes open for people who were journeying, seeking to get deeper into the truth and risking engagement in society to try to establish justice. When they came forward we wondered whether a community with such a raw diversity could hold together. But it was exactly this second grouping which succeeded in forming the creative community to which I now belong.'

PRAYER

Lord God,
You see our rough edges.
– be our Dry Stone Dyker
to use these differences, even the awkwardnesses,
to shape lively stones into a house of your presence,
their rough edges so aligned that they add strength to one
another.

It is of your grace that we are not made from one mould. For you,
who delight in a world of many colours, shapes and sizes, delight
also in the variegated colours, shapes and sizes of humankind.

We give thanks *that no one need feel left out because of difference,*
for your creative touch can make difference an asset; and that no one
need feel left out because of rough edges because these can settle
more effectively into other parts which you build together into a house
for worship and service.

We give thanks *for those on the fringes of church life with lively,*
searching minds who believe that the gospel has more in it than they
find in the church-as-is. You who love them and are prepared to give
fresh gifts to the church through them, make the church ready to receive
new perceptions and be ready to re-form its life in light of these.

We give thanks *that, in our time, people break loose from old*
constraints and go journeying with you into new territories of faith.

May those who seek, find.
We ask it in Jesus Christ's name. Amen.

INTERVIEW WITH FR MARKUS BUCHER IN LINZ (circa 1983)

Q: When you celebrate the eucharist, do you preside?

A: The total company presides. We, all together, say the words of consecration and the communion prayer. In the basic Christian community I am not a priest over the community but a member of the community. A small group would be made responsible for the prayers, and would prepare beforehand and offer them during the service. We do not celebrate in one kind but with bread and wine together.

Q: Do all participate still in the official church, or have some broken away?

A: Some of them participate in parish activities, some have given these up altogether.

Q: What is the relationship of the 'b.c.c.' to the hierarchy in the diocese – do you listen to one another and learn from one another as movement and institution?

A: The bishop of this diocese is a good man, and we have invited him to share in our meetings. He did attend once. We had a very open discussion covering the effects of a hierarchical structure on the life of the church; on women and their place in the church (why should they not be able to become priests?); and on celibacy – matters like that. It was a fruitful meeting.

Q: What makes the community to which you belong different from the traditional parish church?

A: In the smaller community (25 adults and almost 20 children) it is possible to enter into relationships with one another which go much deeper. It is also a community in which everyone can participate, as it is more democratically than hierarchically developed. It is more politically aware. The bible and the eucharist are very important for members. Celebrating the eucharist in the way we do has meant that people have rediscovered its meaning. The fresh use of the bible has brought people alive to it as never before.

PRAYER

Holy Spirit of God,
You will not let us be. You stir us up. You disturb our complacency.
And when you find us eager and willing, you put a new spirit in us
and lead us in new ways. Thanks be to you who test us and tease us
and make us restless to make growth to the measure of the full
stature of Christ.

We give thanks today for new communities, born 'from below',
who seek to live the faith imaginatively in order to declare it truthfully.

We give thanks that the eucharist is being rediscovered as nourish-
ment for struggles to give concrete expression to our prayers for the
coming of the Kingdom.

We give thanks that the bible is alive as never before, providing
the dynamic of insight into God's ways which keeps people travelling
hopefully.

We give thanks that people are rediscovering the place of small
cells, where people can share deeply and discern fresh ways of
obedience, in the building up of the Body.

We pray that this new life may not be spurned by official
authorities, and that the traditional church may not be spurned by
those who take new ways; but that there may be collaboration in
seeking to understand your will for our time, and adventurousness
in implementing it
all to your glory and the blessing of humanity. Amen.

A CHURCH 'BORN FROM BELOW'

THE first European Congress of basic christian communities was held in Holland in 1983. It was brought into being through the initiative of Dutch members.

It was brilliantly organised. A specially long holiday weekend was chosen. This allowed communities to meet as such – those in work, the unemployed, children together. Representatives from other countries were thus inserted into living communities where they could get the feel of their life, work and worship. On the Saturday all gathered in Amsterdam, where Bishop Mendez Arceo of Mexico and others spoke of developments in their own countries. On Sunday there was a return to each of the b.c.c.s for a gathering-up meeting, including critical reflection on the whole event, a sharing of different forms of experience in different countries, a common meal, worship to which many contributed prayers and thoughts; and a eucharist where the children served the elements to the people. In the afternoon Margaret and I were invited to represent Britain at a first 'Collective' of representatives of b.c.c.s in Western Europe (Eastern Europeans would join later) whose work would be to assess Congresses and plan ahead.

The b.c.c. into which we were welcomed was the Salland community. 'How did it come into being?' we asked.

'One of our number phoned some friends and also put an advertisement in the local paper which said, "I want to find out what it is to live the Christian faith in these times. I believe that the official church is hindering rather than helping me. Would anyone join me in a search to discover what it is to live the Christian faith today?" In no time 30 people responded. Now we are 70 and have had to divide into two to retain the depth of relationship which has been a highly important characteristic of our form of church.'

PRAYER

Lord God,
You are the great Disturber.
You shook Moses out of the torpor of sheepminding and, with Zipporah, sent him, a wanted man in Egypt, to accomplish an impossible task.

You stirred John the Baptist to face the hostility of Herod and Herodias and Scribes and Pharisees and to call an expectant people to prepare for a new Coming.

You made Jesus restless with the outward observance of religious laws and prescriptions, and made him the bearer of new life to humanity.

Give us the courage to move in your name from religious practices which fail to express the new life Christ came to bring, from conventions which have outlived their usefulness, from traditions which have lost their living quality; so that the church in every age may represent joyous discovery of good news for young and old.

We pray for basic christian communities, with their promise of church renewal in worship, in bible study, in engagement for justice.
May we not seek, in our day, to put new wine into old bottles but remember that the new wine of the gospel will keep bursting old containers.
Show us what fresh and flexible wineskins must replace the old.

We ask it in Jesus Christ's name. Amen.

WELL READ

SHE was a shy African woman. When teased by her loud-mouthed neighbour, she was tongue-tied, unable to produce a ready answer to her taunts.

The reason for the scorn which was heaped upon her was the place that she gave to the bible. Not only did she read it regularly. If any problem or dilemma faced her which she found difficult to cope with, she would go into her hut, turn to passages which she thought might help her, meditate upon them, then emerge to deal with the situation.

Things came to a head.

In front of the others, the neighbour took her to task.

'There are all kinds of books in the world which can help us find how to live,' she said. 'Yet you turn to just one – always the same one. *Why*, tell me why – why this *one* book?'

At last the woman's tongue was loosened.

The words came: 'Other books I read,' she said. 'This book reads me.'

REFLECTION

Lord, you have searched me and known me,
You know when I sit down and when I rise up,
you discern my thoughts from a distance.
You search out my going and my lying down
and are acquainted with all my ways ...

~ Psalm 139 ~

PRAYER

Lord of all life,
You see me through and through. That scares and heartens me.
Who I really am is laid bare before you. You penetrate all the
layers of my defences to reach the core of my being. My pretences
evaporate under your gaze. The real me is exposed. Others I can
deceive, but not you.
I cringe at what you see: the mask of obedience under which
self-interest lurks; the appearance of responsibility which conceals
self-serving aims; a cover-up of inaction with words; a cover-up of
want of thought with action; the evasion of demanding tasks and
demanding relationships; and sins and faults for which I cannot
even express contrition because they are hidden from me.
Reach to the depths of my being, I pray, and cleanse me thoroughly
of my sin.
Your all-seeing gaze also heartens me. You see in me not only one
who has let you down, but as one for whom Jesus Christ died, whom he
represents before you face. His acceptance of me gives me confidence.
His indwelling transforms my life. Because of him I can trust in your
forgiveness and learn to live differently.
All this I would not know but for the bible.
Thanks be to God. Amen.

BIBLICAL NOURISHING

IN Rosyth Parish Church it took about three years to gain the kirk session's agreement that we should start every meeting with bible study. But once that conviction took hold it was difficult to limit the bible study to one hour – it was discovered to be so relevant to the life and work of a Dockyard town! Testimony to this reality and to the variety of gifts released is given in notes I recorded in 1959:

'Over the years the kirk session has gained a new solidarity and sense of community through this submission of its life to the Scriptures. There has been a new honesty of approach. Elders who hesitantly expressed doubts and queries have had their tongues properly loosed when these were seen to be widely shared by other elders. Many things which had been accepted without question are now being looked at afresh .... Elders are gaining an enlarged sympathy for those who are beyond the bounds of the church, realising that the church folk and others have similar difficulties concerning faith and life.

'They have developed a new regard for one another as for people differently gifted for bible study. This man* has a gift of clarity of exposition, his neighbour a gift of doubt which makes us look twice at things we might otherwise assume lightly. One has a gift of insight – he seems to get to the heart of the matter at once: another has a fruitful stubbornness, refusing to be easily convinced. This man has the capacity to see swiftly how a biblical passage illuminates working life, his neighbour is able to give humble testimony to what a passage has meant in his own life. A kirk session meeting is now one at which the ordained minister can certainly at times instruct in terms of his special authorisation and equipment, but is at other times instructed out of the manifold gifts of the church in the world. Over the years this builds up to maturity; and produces the habit of seeking to understand the life of this present age and to deal with it biblically.

'By the grace of the Holy Spirit the bible does unfold. It breaks like bread. It nourishes and rejoices.'

[*At that time women were still not eligible to be members, as they are now.]

REFLECTION

*The bible seems a strange book to many, difficult to make sense of
except in selected passages. It speaks of different perceptions people
in different cultures and different centuries have had of the way God
works in history. It is marred by the actions of those who do the most
dastardly deeds in God's name. It is illuminated by true responses
which teach following generations the way to live. We must struggle
with the texts, calling on the Holy Spirit to open up their meaning,
paying attention to the questions and perceptions of those who strive
as we do to get at the truth, that they and we may* live *that truth in
our day.*

*Why did God make these clues to the divine nature and purposes
over the centuries so awkward and contradictory? Maybe it is an act
of grace. Jesus spoke in parables; and illiterates and the most learned
were put on an equal footing, equally having to struggle to get at the
truth hidden in each (or to take avoiding action!). As people wrestled
with his teaching they grew and matured. If God did our thinking for
us, we would not be fitted to grow into the stature and maturity of
Jesus Christ and share his life and his glory (see Ephesians 4).*

*So God tests our mettle by the way life's purpose and our part in
it is communicated.*

PRAYER

God the Lord,
   May your Word be a lamp to our feet and a light on our path.
                                                              Amen.

DOING JUSTICE TO SCRIPTURE

BY word of mouth and through their written documents, Italian basic christian communities helped me to understand their journeys. These had features in common. That applies to their experiences of handling the Scriptures.

First, people will come to the point where they say: 'The priest/ pastor treats the bible as his book, selecting what he wants and inter-preting it as he chooses. It is our book, the book of the church. We are going to discover for ourselves what its message is.'

After some time they will criticise their own approach: 'We are being fundamentalist. That is not good enough. The texts of the bible were set down at different times, in different cultures, in different forms, for different purposes. We have not been fair to the material we have been wrestling with.'

The upshot often is that each member will be asked to consult a different commentary and bring insights and challenges to the small communities. This may go on for some time. It can often prove to be an enlightening stage. But a point will be reached where they say, 'We used to sit at the feet of priests and pastors. Now we are sitting at the feet of commentators. We are still not making the bible a resource, related to our own experience, which nourishes our lives and directs our action in this world.'

The way through can be to ensure that a theological scholar or scholars join the community. Such people need to be guaranteed to be good listeners and non-dominating. Then they can learn and share. If scholars are thin on the ground, main perceptions and queries can be stored up and presented to one or more once per month to check on the group's insights.

Thus disciplines for living and scholarly disciplines interpenetrate and fertilise one another.

REFLECTION

Your decrees are wonderful
therefore my soul keeps them.
The unfolding of your words gives light
it imparts understanding to the simple.
~ Psalm 119: 129,130 ~

PRAYER

Lord God,
We praise and bless you that, in our day, we see what many
prophets and righteous people longed to see but were prevented from
seeing:
> – *all kinds of people search the scriptures and get light for their*
>   *daily lives;*
> – *scholars are prepared to gain insights from those whose*
>   *disciplines are in living and suffering, and to contribute their*
>   *own perceptions humbly, acting within communities of faith;*
> – *the bible is made accessible in many languages and in modern*
>   *texts.*
We bless you for those who invest energy and time in translation
work; in expository teaching; in finding easily-read typesets; in
printing and distribution: so that the scriptures are accessible to
those who would turn to them.
We bless you that the scriptures provide a springboard for trans-
forming this world.

'The Word was with God and the Word was God .... What has come
into being through him was life, and the life was the light of all people.'
~ John 1: 1, 4 ~

We believe this scripture: thanks be to God. Amen.

THE RISK INVOLVED IN INTERPRETING SCRIPTURE

THE following is part of an interview with a Baptist pastor in Rome in 1974. He was leading representatives of the basic christian communities in that city in a day of Bible study on the Year of Jubilee, comparing and contrasting that with the coming Holy Year (*Annus Jubilaei*) which seemed to be designed to minister to the power and status of the Vatican. A question concerned this unusual Roman Catholic/Baptist tie-up.

A: It was in 1971 that our community linked up with people who might be called 'Dissenting Catholics'. We found we had much to share through our common concern about the Bible – and it was in this field that I think we Baptists have had a special contribution to give. We are all together in this venture as a Baptist community.

Q: You seem to make a strong connection between biblical insights and political action.

A: Yes, but also this is something that has to be watched. The two must not be tied up too directly but of course each relates to the other. The Roman Catholic Church in the past picked bits of the Bible to support its position. As we take a new direction, we could pick the bits of the Bible which suit ours! We must be very critical of our use of the Bible and not just turn to favourite passages which support our case.

Q: How can you prevent that happening?

A: Now it must be the people themselves who discover the deep meaning of the biblical testimony and the reality of the work they are called to in the world. We (clergy) must no longer impose.

But this still means that risks are to be taken in working this out. We believe we must fight for justice in the world, and so we oppose the Vietnam War: yet we have not all been absolutely clear that this is demanded by our faith! We have come to believe that if standing up for human beings should cost us our faith, then we must risk our faith. But really, in our hearts, we believe, we are with Jesus Christ in this kind of fight.

PRAYER

God the Father,

Yours was a high-risk strategy. We human beings have dashed your hopes time and again. We have warred with each other. We have warred with the creation. We have been preoccupied with our own interests and have let your beloved human family and your beloved natural order suffer. How your heart must have bled down the centuries to see the betrayal of your best hopes.

God the Son,

You diced with sin and death to give us a fresh start. Was it worth it? Was it worth it when you see our continuing unwillingness to take your way, our reluctance to spend our lives for others and be ready to act with as little certainty of the outcome as you had in Gethsemane?

God the Holy Spirit,

You strive with our spirits to tempt us to move out of familiar and safe territory, trusting only in your strong hand to hold us up if we fail and fall. But we love our securities and cling to them. Our inclination to be apostles, journeying into the unknown, attentive there to find your will, gets stifled.

Yet you keep looking to us, Father, Son and Holy Spirit – not going back to the drawing board to fashion more dependable partners; and from time to time you rejoice to see your friends and followers taking the risks of faith, prepared to lose even their grip on you if that is the risk required to follow where you seem to lead.

Give them your blessing: and make them a sign of encouragement to all of us to hazard our lives for the Kingdom's sake.

We ask it in your name as Trinity. Amen

A CHURCH BUILDING ITSELF UP IN LOVE

IT was in the Ipil diocese of Mindanao in the Philippines in 1982 that I came across one of the most constructive relationships established between professional theologians and those who were 'living the faith at ground level'.

In the diocese there were 1200 basic christian communities. Each week they gathered round the bible, looking for light to help them deal with the oppression from which they suffered under the Marcos dictatorship, plagued as they were on the one hand by poverty and on the other by threats of armed gangs. Work on the bible was prepared for two or three months ahead. This is how it was done.

The start was with peasants and workers. They would identify concrete issues in situations they faced which needed to be addressed. With their growing knowledge of the bible they would identify texts which might help them to deal with these issues from a faith perspective. Only then would the professionals come in. Almost inevitably they would be greatly enlightened by hearing of the texts of the bible which the people considered to be relevant. They might then go on to say: 'You suggest consulting this part of the bible. But are you aware that that other part seems to speak in flat contradiction of it?'

'Then we must study both,' would come the reply.

Thereafter they work together. It becomes a matter not of specialists building up the church, but of the whole church building itself up in love (Ephesians 4: 16), preparing ahead biblical resources for nourishing and directing lives.

PRAYER

God the Lord,

Enable us to love the world as Jesus loved it

- *not treating it as alien territory when he made it his home;*
- *not downgrading it as if it were anything other than God's handiwork;*
- *not turning our backs on it as if true life were found elsewhere;*
- *not despising indigenous insights which can often instruct the church universal; nor claiming that these insights are Christian perceptions, to comfort ourselves;*
- *not avoiding the raw and rough elements to be encountered in the world;*
- *not blinding ourselves to the power-play of powers-that-be but showing genuine love by*
  - *getting to know by research and analysis the dynamic structures of this real world which you, Lord God, affirmed;*
  - *reaching by prayer into the heart of events to give you, our Lord, purchase on them;*
  - *gaining experience by direct involvement;*
  - *listening to all who 'can say what it is like';*
  - *sharing with others who have special skills and knowledge*
  - *drawing on our biblical faith;*
        that kingdoms of this world
might become the Kingdom of our Lord and of his Christ
    and that we may play our part in the transformation
        that he might reign for ever and ever. Amen.

A LITTLE CHILD SHALL LEAD THEM

IT was at the Dessauerhaus-gemeinde in Frankfurt. The gathering lasted for most of the day as is often the case when members of a basic christian community meet on a Sunday.

Different members led in prayer and in bible reading. Then to reflect on the scriptures, those present were divided into groups: children, adolescents, young adults, older people. Margaret and I looked at one another and sighed. Generations had so much to give one another – why separate them off at this point?

We were wrong. Back they came in due time to a plenary assembly. The groups had each appointed one of their number to share with others how the scriptural text related to life as they would have to lead it through the following week.

I do not speak German. Margaret did. But it was as clear to me as to her that when the representative of the children's group took the floor, attention was given to him in a measure denied to the others. That day the Word of God for that company was certainly spoken by a child.

I asked how old he was. Nine years I was informed. The contribution came from the eight to nine year old group.

REFLECTION

*A child has been born to us, a son given to us
authority rests upon his shoulders; and he is named
Wonderful Counsellor, Mighty God
Everlasting Father, Prince of Peace.
His authority shall grow continually
and there shall be endless peace
for the throne of David and his kingdom.
He will establish and uphold it with justice
and with righteousness
from this time onward and forevermore.*
~ Isaiah 9: 6, 7 ~

PRAYER

Lord God, you turn the tables on human wisdom.
  – *To establish a city which has foundations, where you are
    architect and coping stone, you call one family to move out of
    Ur of the Chaldees and invite them to journey into the unknown.*
  – *To establish a line which will bear the knowledge of your saving
    power down the centuries, you make the bearers almost barren,
    and provide for them late and difficult births.*[*]
  – *When danger threatens your chosen ones, you raise up unlikely
    people: Moses the 'Wanted Man', Rahab the harlot, David the
    shepherd boy.*
  – *To face down great empires and establish a kingdom of peace
    and justice ... a child is born.*

*Let us, we pray, keep alert to the ways you work when you make the
seemingly small and weak into bearers of your promise that 'all shall
be well and all manner of things shall be well', to your glory and
praise for ever and ever. Amen.*

[*Sarah, Rebecca, Rachel]

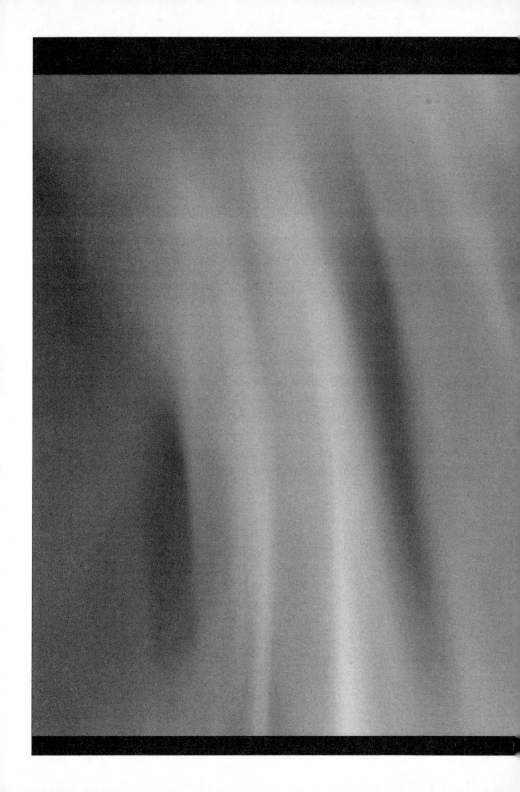

3

IN GOD'S ENTERPRISE

Dunblane
Breaking barriers
Ecumenical experiments

A PROPHETIC RESPONSE

WE had been in Rosyth Parish Church for 12 years and were beginning to be urged to think of offering this or that alternative service when Dr Robert Mackie asked if he could meet with us.

Seven churches, he told us, and several interdenominational bodies had come to the point where they were prepared to have a house in common as a base for witness and service in Scotland. At that point of time Roman Catholics could not come in with the others but showed genuine goodwill.

A row of eighteenth century cottages along one side of the Cathedral Square in Dunblane was due for demolition but could possibly be saved. The site had historical significance. Blane and his monks had come in AD 600 or 602 and established their community near the top of the hill at the foot of which the houses nestled. From there the Celtic mission extended to the surrounding countryside. The monks brought skills not only for gospel proclamation, but for ameliorating the life of the people through healing, better farming methods, craftsmanship in wood and stone.

'To be fair to you,' said Dr Mackie, 'I must present the whole picture. We need someone to head up the enterprise. Your names have been prominently before us. We have at present no money for such an appointment, nor for restoring the buildings.'

Margaret quietly said, 'That's for us!'

At the time she was getting a maximum dose of radiotherapy for cancer in the Western General Hospital, Edinburgh. She did not know whether she would still be alive at the end of that year.

PRAYER

Lord God,
        who are a community of love,
  today we give you thanks and praise for those who act ahead of
their time, furnishing future generations with stepping stones to move
forward and to minister more effectively to national communities –
thus preparing a way for a more convincing expression of that one,
holy, catholic, apostolic church for which Jesus Christ gave his life.

    Forbid that we embrace the vision without the venturing.
    Enable us in our day to make new paths in untrodden ways.

We give you thanks and praise
    for those who are prepared to act prophetically
    in all the disadvantages of circumstance
    and against all the odds,
    trusting you to supply life-giving energy
    when the body would seem unable to bear the strain,
    in confidence that you can provide for us
    beyond all that we might ask or think
    according to the power which works in us.

Lord God,
      if you call me to tasks which are beyond me,
  grant me not to measure them against the strength I possess
but against the strength you provide – remembering that I can do all
things through Christ who strengthens me.

    So let me think the unthinkable,
      bear the unbearable
   and venture where there is no sure path for my feet:
   in the name of the one who walked on water. Amen

HIDDEN TREASURE

IN 1959 the row of 18th century domestic dwellings on one side of the cathedral square in Dunblane was given to the churches to provide a common base for their outreach in Scotland. The buildings were derelict and had to be restored professionally. But the wild ground at the back was tackled by a World Council of Churches' Work Camp in 1960.

From the back door of the house about a dozen steps led upwards and then stopped, giving way to earth. The campers tackled the earth – and found more steps underneath, continuing upward to the point where they reached a wall covered with ivy. The ivy was cleared. First a window, ecclesiastical in type, came into view, then a door, finally an arched room dripping with moisture from the earth in which it was set. Instinctively work campers called it 'the chapel'. Local historian, Miss Barty, had noted records of the existence of 'the Old Chapel' which did not fit the character of other cellars found in the area. This could be it. The character of the building suggested a time contemporaneous with the thirteenth century bishop's palace.

The roof at the higher level was unearthed and cemented. Amateur attempts to tank in the building failed. Meantime architect Eric Stevenson had furnished the chapel brilliantly with a standing cross round which to gather, a table altar which could be used at the front, back or side, and lights scattered over the roof reminding worshippers of the angels of the churches in the book of Revelation, placed like stars in the hand of the Son of Man.

Before the professional tanking in, a water diviner had been hired to identify all sources of water which came from the surrounding banking. Having done his job he went across to the table altar saying, 'Do you know you have a body buried under here?', indicating with his wands an East-West ecclesiastical burial.

The small chapel of Columba in Iona was one in which people could pray in the presence of the saints' relics, when that was their resting place. Could the Dunblane chapel be a gift from the undivided church to the reuniting church, where people could pray in the presence of the bones of some unknown saint?

REFLECTION

Do not be afraid; I am the first and the last and the
living one. I was dead and, see, I am alive for ever and
ever; and I have the keys of Death and of Hades ... As for
the mystery of the seven stars that you saw in my right hand
and the seven golden lampstands:
the seven stars are the angels of the seven churches
and the seven lampstands are the seven churches.
~ Revelation 1: 17, 18, 20 ~

PRAYER

Lord God,
We give thanks for the gifts of the past to the future. We give
thanks for pioneers and prophets who ventured beyond familiar
territory and struck out a way for others to follow; who did not
receive The Promise – for you had prepared a better way that they
without us should not be made perfect.

> *Enable us to play our part in our day, getting nourishment for*
> *our faith from their example and tackling our own assignments,*
> *to your glory.*

We pray for those who died feeling that they were failures, yet
were like seed cast into the earth which, in its time, became fruitful.
May we learn from the Suffering Servant not to apply the world's
standards; but to realise that, whatever we do trusting in Jesus
Christ can be gathered into a large initiative and whatever we fail
to do can be covered by a comprehensive forgiveness.

> *It is for you to say what gives glory to your name.*
> *It is enough if we, in our time, seek to be faithful to our calling.*

Grant, we pray, that the churches may be like lampstands which
throw light on the past and on the future, illuminating treasures of the
past which can enrich life today and showing us the way to Jesus
Christ who comes from the future with new treasures in his torn hands.
In his name we ask it. Amen.

THE EARLY DAYS: 1960

FRESH from the pub, swaying on the pavement opposite us, Addie delivered his verdict with all the authority of the inebriate. 'It'll no' work,' he declared as we Work Campers sweated to unload heavy building stones from the parked lorry. 'Yer Scottish Churches Hooses thing'll niver come tae naethin'.'

But the wisdom of the wise is foolishness with God.

Work Campers transformed the back area and Monaghan and Company rehabilitated the row of Houses for their new purpose, under the imaginative planning of Eric Stevenson. Allison Harvey brought her vision and with it the gift of Maisie Masson (commending her with some diffidence because of their close companionship – it was as if the Queen, giving away the Koh-I-Noor, apologised that it had not been dusted that day). My wife Margaret charmed people with the grace of her presence so that they felt welcome from the moment they came in the door. Jack and Betty Stevenson, Archie and May Craig built into the enterprise their love, prayer, service – and Leighton House and the Flower Garden of Scottish Churches House. Marie Brotherston in the kitchen made sure that Blue Angels returned to their respective countries furnished with a much more vivid grasp of English than any language school could have provided, able to tell of the 'collieshangies' they had worked their way through and what had 'fair scunnered' and 'fair chuffed' them about Scotland. The arrival of Gillian Carver added strength and imagination. Fittingly, Bill and Barbara Baker rounded off a life-investment of support with the gift of the new ecumenical library.

Decisive parts were played by Neville Davidson and Robert Mackie in the total enterprise. When the new Scottish Churches Council came into being in 1964 Lord Wemyss chaired it through its first years.

In all this we were not sure whether we could pull anything off. But then neither was Abraham (imagine the profanities of a long-distance lorry driver given the instructions which provided his only guide for the journey!)

REFLECTION

How long is a piece of string? How many hands are needed to establish an ecumenical enterprise? To name names is to identify a vast spectrum of gifts and givers.

Consider the great range of gifts needed to bring into being an enterprise of the churches together, which will speak to all of them and will speak for all of them. One must mention name upon name upon name upon name.

Contributions are made at all levels. Only thus could a place designed to be a springboard for the churches together come into being and become operational in Scotland.

Think of the list of occupations in Ecclesiasticus 38 and the conclusion:

'All these ... are skillful in their own work. Without them no city can be inhabited, there would be no settling, no travelling ... they maintain the fabric of the world ....'

PRAYER

Lord God,

We give you thanks for those who work without acclaim, often without adequate thanks – whom you honour and bless and love:

We acclaim the work of those,

> *who barrow sand and mix cement*
> *who dig trenches and mend pipes*
> *who carry bricks and stones for building*
> *who dispose of rubbish*
> *who grow vegetables*
> *who cook meals*
> *who wash and dust and iron*
> *who drive lorries and huge transports:*

that projects which are planned with care and designed with flair
> *may be fulfilled to your honour and glory. Amen.*

BREAKING FREE

THE last event in 1969 in Scottish Churches House before our move to Geneva and the World Council of Churches was a week-long conference of lay people. Twenty-five Roman Catholics and 25 Protestants had Willie Barclay and Bernard Haring let loose among them. No programme was prepared beforehand. That was allowed to develop out of the gathering's internal dynamic.

The concluding event was a Mass in the local chapel, with Dr Haring as the celebrant. It had been agreed beforehand that Protestants could participate but not partake.

But when the service came to the point which could have been a point of division, Dr Haring's face lit up like the face of an angel and he threw his arms wide in invitation. Whatever his mind had suggested in the abstract, when the bit came to the bit he could not divide those who, over the week, had become one community in Christ.

Years later we met in Birmingham. I asked him how he now looked on that action. The essence of his reply was:

'When we consider how to move forward I find two things particularly important: Tradition and Spirit.

'We can examine the evidence on which people based conclusions which shaped the tradition; then at evidence which accumulated later: and ask whether the traditional interpretation is justified by the total evidence. That makes tradition a living source of faith instead of a dead weight round our necks.

'We must also make ourselves available to the Holy Spirit. If, as a result, we are brought beyond positions we previously held, we must take ourselves particularly severely to task. Was our response really at the urging of the Spirit or could it be traced to superficial emotionalism, avoidance of hard realities, pressure of circumstances, some confusion of spirit or such?'

'What about that Mass in Dunblane in 1969?' I asked.

'That? *That* was the Holy Spirit.'

PRAYER

Living Lord of all life,
You ask us to take risks of faith. That means stepping out beyond the certainties. The certainties, established over centuries, are what undergird our life. They nourish that life day by day. They make sense of our birth and death and everything in between. They are a sure foundation.

So why should we step out?
We bless you that Jesus Christ showed us that the ultimate certainty lies not in words but in his life; that that life moves to heal and bless the world: and that if we would be part of it, we also must be prepared to move, guided by the Spirit.

For our only final certainty is you, our God.
We ask your forgiveness for wanting to hedge our bets as if we could not trust Jesus Christ to be the Way, the Truth and the Life. We know that by drawing back when we should act boldly we hinder the advance of the Kingdom.

We give thanks for those who venture, not recklessly but thought-fully, for the Kingdom's sake. Especially we pray for those who are persecuted and ostracised in consequence. We who can move through the world's jungles because they hacked a way ahead, bless you for their courage.

So help us to recognise what is of the Spirit and to distinguish that from what stems from unregulated impulse. Help us in consequence to act with firmness in spite of all our fears and forebodings
that others who follow may bless us because we also
have cleared a highway in the desert for our God,
as did John the Baptist
and that they may walk with safety who walk your way. Amen.

BREAKING BARRIERS

The Ecumenical Association of Third World Theologians (EATWOT) deliberately turned its back on counterparts in the West – not in hostility but in an attempt to concentrate on the resources indigenous to Third World countries, which were so often overlooked and neglected in Western theology. They succeeded in developing fresh angles and emphases. What was harder to do was to shuffle off Western ways of thinking with which their minds had been impregnated. It took the creative insights of women to make a substantive change as EATWOT developed over the years.

The time arrived when EATWOT members were ready for an encounter with Western colleagues. That encounter took place in Geneva. A concluding service of Holy Communion gathered into it the thoughts and aspirations of participants expressed over the days of shared experience.

Seven women presided. No one whom I questioned knew who among them was ordained and who was not. What we all knew was that they were 'orderly appointed' by the company – which was as representative of the church catholic as you could find anywhere.

In the approach to the sacrament, a prayer embraced the communion of saints this and that side of death. Those who had died were invited to be present with the company assembled, in words such as these: 'Oscar Romero, we are making room for you to come among us and share with us in this sacrament. Jesus Christ is here, you are with Christ, we make you welcome with him at this feast. We rejoice to have you with us, you who are risen among your people.'

Other names were called out, still others mentioned silently. The room filled to overflowing with the church, militant and triumphant.

REFLECTION

The Spirit and the Bride say, 'Come'.
Let everyone who hears say, 'Come'.
Let whoever is thirsty come:
that all who want may take the water of life freely.
~ Revelation 22: 17 ~

There are times when the call to take the water of life freely is so commanding, the invitation so pressing, that barriers in the way are brushed aside. What results is not disorderly. It expresses the order of the Holy Spirit.

In their actions towards AD 2000 the Iona Community and ecumenical agencies in Britain invite support for a proposal that certain events and certain places be recognised as appropriate for sharing Holy Communion across separated traditions. This would be in line with the biblical invitation to take the water of life freely. It would also take account of difficulties faced by those in official positions in the churches, by proposing limited steps whose effects could be assessed before any further move should be contemplated.

We are at a time when thoughtful breakthroughs are needed. We are at a time when tradition needs to be respected. One way to respect it is to use it as a springboard, not a cage.

What EATWOT did was not done defiantly. It simply marked the point at which it had arrived in its journey. No more appropriate action to sum up the consultation could have been imagined.

PRAYER

Lord God,
You have led us to this day. New light has been shed on all our traditions. We have more community in the truth than we have had for many centuries.
Lead us in your mercy to the fullness of your will for us
in Christ's name. Amen.

LET GO

ADVICE which hierarchies and bureaucracies need to hear is, 'Let go! God will provide what is needed'.

At the time of the celebration of the first anniversary of the success of the revolution in Nicaragua, I stayed in the barrio 'Ciudad Sandino', in a small Jesuit community which lived at the level of the people. My resource person was Paco who had been my contact with communities in Paraguay when he was serving there. I asked him what it was like for priests to find basic Christian communities developing in the area. He said:

'We were scared. We were really scared. We saw all that we had been trained and ordained for disappearing into the people and thought that nothing might be left for us. Was preaching our task? The people building one another up in understanding of the Bible and the faith through the experiences of seeking to live it in a pressured situation each day, were far better preachers than we could aspire to be. Was worship then our responsibility? The people lifting to God their struggles and sufferings and praising God with joy and hope in the midst of it all, developed worship full of reality for which we as ordained could offer no substitute. At least the Mass was in our control? We very soon became convinced that it was the action of the people together. We thought there would be nothing left for us. We seriously considered the question whether we should try to pull things back into our own court before they got lost altogether.'

'And what did you do?' I asked.

'We just had enough grace to let go,' said Paco.

'And what happened?'

'In no time at all the people had given back a place to us not over them but with them. We have rediscovered ministry together.'

PRAYER

Lord God,

The great gifts are ones we do not need to protect, for you secure them for us. So let us trust in you to give what is needful that your church may fulfil its mission to the ends of the earth and the end of time, even when that threatens our securities.

We give thanks for the function of ordination – that the church sets aside, trains, mandates a particular form of ministry for the good of the whole Christian community; and that there are those whom it releases to undertake that service in the confidence that they have a modest part to play

 – *and we confess times when the function to serve the church has been distorted into power over the membership, diminishing instead of strengthening the people's ministry.*

We give thanks for the gifts of the Spirit distributed among the people which enable them to be a praising, praying, proclaiming community of love; and that the most vulnerable and least articulate have ministries to fulfil which rejoice your heart

 – *and we confess both an unreadiness ourselves to use these gifts to the full, and also to honour them in others when they seek to bring them into play. Then we break the bruised reed and dowse the smoking flax which we should gently blow into flame. By your grace forgive us.*

Lord God,

Make us eager to release one another into ministries which will help the world to appreciate where the true source of life lies, which will heal and bless humankind and safeguard and enhance the whole order of creation.

 – *Let those of us who hold office not hold back your gifted church for fear of losing personal power and position,*
        for it is when we are weak that we are strong. Amen.

POLL TAX

I WOULD have had less to pay under the Community Charge (Poll Tax) provisions. But poor people were being crushed. I knew that the tax had to be opposed. Protest marches were not enough. The courts offered another option. I knew nothing about the law in relation to the tax. I knew nothing about court procedure. I had to learn by doing.

So I went to the Poll Tax Office in Stirling and asked them how to oppose the measure. They gave me a straight answer. If I refused to return even the signing-on form I would be summoned, would get the chance to make my case before the local sheriff; and would have to take it from there, depending on the verdict.

I did so. The verdicts in the Sheriff Court and later the Court of Session went against me – but I had at least been given the chance to argue that the law supporting the Poll Tax was bad law and should be denied legitimacy. Decisions in both courts were mainly based on technicalities, so I was able to put forward a case to the European Court. That Court was prepared to give me a hearing. But at that point the Government abandoned the tax. My immediate response was to pay all the back-tax and the tax due for the current year.

When the Poll Tax was applied to England, a group of Christian resisters came into being, including professional theologians. We met in Durham and had got well into the work of developing a theology of resistance when the Government stood the tax down. Theology and action proved to be mutually instructive.

PRAYER

God the Lord,

*Every authority must bow to your authority. To you, all govern-
ments are subject. You ask of them righteous dealings. You also
require your people to bring back earthly authorities, when they
stray from that path, to true ways, just laws, fair taxes*
*– so help us to choose the right fights and to see them through to
the end.*

God the Lord,

*We, who acknowledge you, are still sinful. We may show bad
judgment, be motivated by private and personal prejudices, start
something we do not see through to the finish. We need compass-
bearings to keep us on the right track*
*– so help us to draw imaginatively on the resources of bible and
theology.*

God the Lord,

*We remember with sympathy any whose official position requires
them to administer laws and practices against which their soul
revolts. Enable them to find means to mitigate the worst effects of
bad laws, and, by the way in which they interpret them, give maximum weight to positive features. May they know that they have
sympathisers who appreciate what it is like to be caught in systems.*

God the Lord,

*Your beloved poor have to bear the brunt of so many political
decisions. Help us to use what opportunities are open to us to
apply pressure to secure fair treatment for them. Enable us to see
that it is a spiritual task to learn how decisions at a high level are
made and implemented: that we may not only wish the poor well
but take measures to ensure that they get their fair share of the
human inheritance and opportunity to contribute creatively to the
world's development.*
We ask it in Jesus Christ's name. Amen.

GAMBLING WITH LIFE

JACQUES Chonchol, Minister of Agrarian Reform in Salvador Allende's government in Chile, answered my question by dodging it. I represented the World Council of Churches. The heart of the interview was the take-over of agricultural land.

I had visited three areas of agrarian reform about 200 kilometres south of Santiago. Conversations with peasants who now worked the land as their own, revealed an impressive change in their mentality as well as in their material situation. Their forebears had for centuries been treated as hewers of wood and drawers of water. From nowhere it seemed they had developed gifts of leadership, capacities for communal initiative. I have heard of deserts which had not had rain for fifty years. When rains came the deserts blossomed. It was like that in Chile.

At times the state took over farms and divided them among the workers. At times the workers organised and took over the farms themselves, while the state came in later and confirmed their ownership. Jacques Chonchol clearly preferred the latter. Peasants who organised a take-over would have developed skills for acting as a community and for managing the land they seized. He must have felt that, in his official position, he had to give equal emphasis to both methods of redistribution. But his unstated preference was clear.

The vast *latifundias* which were appropriated contained great stretches of land which had not been cultivated or put to any alternative use, but yet had been denied to the peasants. I learned of landlords who had broken up their agricultural machinery when the land was seized, leaving the peasants only basic tools to work with. In spite of this, at the end of the first year, they had increased productivity.

It was a revolution with too much promise in it. So it was bloodily squashed.

PRAYER

Lord God,
What a spirit you have put in human beings!
Did your eyes go round with delight, did you clap your hands and
tap your feet when Miriam led the rout after the crossing of the Red
Sea; when Mary sang of promised deliverance for oppressed people;
when your beloved humanity in this century risked life and limb to
establish on the earth truer governments, fairer systems?

Do you rejoice with one another in the Trinity when you see positive
results from the gamble taken breathing your own life into us: your
own daring reflected in the daring of your human family, your own
sense of justice reflected in their fights for justice, your own
community expressed in their common coordinated action to over-
turn false and establish fair structures?

Does your heart leap when you see the poor, once derided and set
aside, claiming the place in the sun which you have prepared for
them: looking to you for light and hazarding their lives to live by that
light?

And does your heart break when you see the bloody response of the
powerful to such action which, they realise, threatens their policies
of domination?

Then Father, Son and Holy Spirit, we can delight in you, and
believe in you and trust our cause to you
        for it is from you that we have learned to love
        and to gamble life at love's insistence. Amen.

CHANGING DIRECTION TO BE CONSISTENT

IN February and March 1995 I was in South Africa at the invitation of Margaret and Colin Legum. Imaginatively they had been prepared to dedicate a house which Margaret's mother had left them as a Columban house. Thanks to the quality of service provided by Rosie, the house-keeper, a basis already existed – it was a house of hospitality and of outreach to meet needs in the area. In the post-apartheid situation, were there other concrete forms of service for which the house could be a base? We set ourselves to find out.

One evening about two dozen representatives from the neighbour-hood, black and white, met to give their advice. They put their finger on several forms of service which they thought relevant. One of these concerned schools.

It had been part of the struggle against apartheid to make schools ungovernable. The whole country had to be made ungovernable while it remained under the old regime if change were to take place. But once Mandela's government was in power, things continued on their old course. How could the situation be turned round? The Columban House was seen as a place to which pupils, teachers and parents could resort to see if a new conviction about disciplined learning could be arrived at by all parties, and ways found to express that conviction in practice.

In Soweto I found a parallel situation. The priest, Dale White, reminded the congregation that he had supported their rent boycott ('rent' included water, electricity, sewage services, not just house). The boycott had achieved its objective. So now it was time to do the exact opposite – to pay rent. If they did not do so, people would stay home-less who should be housed. Changing direction would be a mark of consistency.

REFLECTION

St Paul battered his head against the new teaching. The turn-around on the Damascus Road stemmed from the questioning which lay beneath his hostility. People need to be ready to change course for the sake of truth and right. Consistency in seeking the truth may mean we turn around in our tracks.

Give thought to South Africa:
- *To people who, having prayed and fought to overturn an unjust regime find themselves living in townships in the same unrelieved conditions as before.*
- *To those who are on the receiving end of violence, so that they are driven to despair by the sense that no radical change has taken place with the change of government.*

Pray that people show both patience to co-operate in the slow turnabout of the situation leading to the establishment of a more just society; and the impatience which insists that change take place as rapidly as is consistent with protecting society from breakup.

Give thought:
- *To privileged whites who will find it hard to give up the advantages which they have enjoyed.*
- *Pray that a readiness to surrender unjustly-awarded favours may mark the response they make, in thanksgiving that civil war has been averted.*

Give thought:
- *To those in positions of responsibility in government, faced by the dilemmas posed by the need both for reconciliation and a just dealing with past transgressions.*

Pray that they may find the right balance between insisting that crimes be punished and that forgiveness accompany the punishment.

We ask all this in Jesus Christ's name. Amen.

ECUMENICAL SHARING

I HAPPENED to call on a member of the congregation around school lunch time in Rosyth in the 1950s. The daughter of the house arrived back crying her eyes out, bruised, dishevelled, with dirty clothes. 'What now?' asked her mother. Between sobs the lass answered that, as she had been passing the Roman Catholic school, some of the pupils had accosted her and asked, 'Are you a Catholic?'

'When I said no, they set on me and bashed me.'

When she got her daughter calmed down and cleaned up, the mother said, 'But you should have said "yes". We belong to the holy, catholic church. The word "catholic" covers all Christians. Remember the creed we say in church. You don't need to let them get on to you. Just answer that you belong to the catholic church.'

At the end of the afternoon, the lady of the house saw me walking past from her window, and called me in.

'You'll never guess what has happened! My daughter came back at the end of the school day in a worse state than ever. I said, "Did you not say you were catholic?"

'"I did," she said through her tears, "but it was the Protestants who asked me this time."'

PRAYER

Lord of the world, lord of the church,
We give you thanks for the Vatican II Council which brought light
and hope to so many people.
We bless you who chose John XXIII, for all his brief tenancy, to
set it in motion; and that he gathered together from around the world
such a perceptive company of Christ's people.
We bless you for the understanding of the church as the People of
God, which allowed new constructive relations to develop between
churches which had been out of kilter with one another; and which
fostered new appreciation of the ministry of the whole membership.
We bless you for the hard work of drafting committees, working
all hours to get clear and agreed statements which could nourish the
church for decades ahead.
We bless you for the openness to other Christians which made the
Council genuinely ecumenical, and for the way in which it pointed
believers to the fullness of union.
We bless you for its openness to the world, which made it clear
that the church does not exist for itself but for the world you love.

Give us grateful hearts for what has thus been done to provide
footholds in history to help us all gain better purchase on your work
throughout the centuries; and see more clearly where it is leading in
our time.

'Since we are surrounded by so great a cloud of witnesses, let us also
lay aside every weight and the sin which clings so closely and let us
run with perseverance the race that is set before us, looking to Jesus
the pioneer and perfecter of our faith.'
~ Hebrews 12: 1, 2 ~

PROPOSALS FOR COVENANTING

WHEN the Proposals for Covenanting were put before the churches I challenged them in a pamphlet entitled 'A Cry'. In it I pointed to the uncritical acceptance of Anglican assumptions and structures; the feeling given of welding together different static blocks of people, instead of releasing a new community into dynamic mission; the treating of ordained ministry (as had been so often the case) as if that could stand in for the whole Priestly People who share in Jesus Christ's ministry to the world. I found the proposed service of unity unimaginative. Its concern was to unite ordained ministries and make that stand for the rest. Instead you could have had a large cathedral where, at the start of the service, representatives of different denominations would sit in separate areas; then when covenanting was confirmed, would move from where they were, greet one another with handshakes and hugs and inter-mingle to form a new congregation, lay and ordained together.

The proposals were voted down by Anglicans (for the worst reasons, in my judgment). I was accused of being anti-ecumenical. But proposals need not provide the true way forward even if they are presented in a genuinely ecumenical spirit by deeply concerned people.

REFLECTION

If one goes against proposals about which people of integrity are convinced, self-questioning is called for. Any proposals for church unity are bound to be flawed – why not accept what might gain assent and build on that?

But proposals for unity might get formal assent and yet fail to gain the conviction of church members. Moreover unity should be for the sake of the world, though also for the sake of the church. It should have in it concern that all people find unity in justice and peace.

PRAYER

Father, Son and Holy Spirit,

Your own unity is a sign for the world of the kind of unity which we should seek. As Father, Son and Holy Spirit you meet us in different ways and meet different needs in us – we rest in the Father, are released into new life by the Son, and are inspired and illuminated by the Spirit.

- *Forgive us whenever we set walls around our nation, making it exclusive; around our race, our colour, our class, our gender, diminishing others in the process.*
- *Forgive us that our nation's unity with other peoples is so often determined by security needs rather than by a responsible outreach to embrace the most vulnerable and insecure.*
- *Forgive us particularly where the church has set a poor example to the nations.*

Already you are moving us into more open water. Keep us moving, we pray, lest the ice close in about us again

and let the growing unity the church experiences be a gift and encouragement to your beloved world, we pray. Amen.

THE BASES AND REFORMATION OF LITURGIES

'WHERE did you get that liturgy? It has elements in it which we would want to recover. Did you make it up yourself?' The questions came from a handful of priests who waited behind to question me when the others had gone.

'The others' belonged to an initiative of Pope John XXIII entrusted to his 'Laity Officer', Sister Rosemary Goldie. The WCC had been invited to appoint 15 people – Orthodox, Lutheran and Reformed – to meet informally with 15 of his own appointees on 'The Church in the Modern World'. This was during Vatican II but was not part of the official programme, though there was an overlap of personnel (notably Monsignor Jerome Hamer, convener of the drafting committee of the Decree on Ecumenism). Klaus von Bismark (maestro in German TV productions) who chaired the first of the gatherings was unable to do so for two succeeding encounters leading up to the Laity Congress in 1967. I was asked to co-chair with Martin Work, a Roman Catholic layman. I was thus given rare opportunity to get an appreciation of the fresh enterprise of Roman Catholicism at that time.

Our joint meetings lasted three to four days. Each day started with sacramental worship. All of us observed the disciplines of that time about partaking. There was a Roman Catholic mass, an Orthodox eucharist, and on the last day I was asked to take a Church of Scotland communion service. It was this last sacrament which stimulated questions by the priests who waited behind. I had to explain that the service they had experienced was simply basically the liturgy of my church, its substance derived from the earliest years of the Christian enterprise, influenced by Celtic and other insights as it moved through history. That basis still left room for a personal touch which could bring home to participants the significance of what they were doing.

Especially now, when different liturgies have been reformed and find themselves occupying so much common ground, it is time to reclaim a common sacramental heritage.

PRAYER

Lord God,
whose Son was content to die
to bring new life
have mercy on your church,
which will do anything you ask,
anything at all,
except die and be reborn.

Lord Christ,
forbid us unity
which leaves us where we are
and as we are;
welded into one company
but extracted from the battle;
engaged to be yours
but not found at your side.

Holy Spirit of God
reach deeper than our inertia and fears:
release us into the freedom of children of God.
Amen

HOLY COMMUNION: RESPONSIBLE OPENNESS

DURING an International Association of Mission Studies conference in Rome, Bishop Patrick Kalilombe was asked to conduct the concluding event – a Mass in the Catacombs. He did so in a way which was fair to his own tradition – and at the same time moved us all forward.

He asked all present to be serious about the discipline of partaking. Those of us who did not belong to his tradition should ask ourselves where our church stood in relation to Roman Catholic practice and, in this regard, in which direction our denomination was moving in its thinking. We should also ask both these questions about our own personal position. In light of the answers we should decide whether we could or could not partake responsibly. Biblical advice was thus restored, namely to examine ourselves and thus decide whether we should. To 'fence tables' and decide who is in and who is out is a poor substitute for this deep self-examination.

In the sacramental service his 'right-hand man' was Rev. Dr Rosario Lugo-Batlle, a Spanish-American Presbyterian woman pastor. Patrick supplied thus a kind of icon of the larger church, embracing all kinds of Christians, into which we are moving.

PRAYER

Father, Son and Holy Spirit,
Our life is rooted in you and gets its coherence and dynamic from you.
You are three, with distinctive features; and you are one, a unity.

- *Change our mentalities, we pray, that we seek not to be conformed to one another but to your rich life.*
- *Give us, we pray, the imagination to overcome obstacles from the past. At the same time give us appreciation of the concern for truth which produced these obstacles: recognising that martyrdom could stem from fanaticism, but also that, at great cost, essential matters of faith could be stoutly affirmed till they became honoured in practice.*
- *Give us, we pray, that acceptance of one another which means we can speak truth to one another and listen sensitively to one another, till your communication of your will for us so invades our conversation that we draw closer to one another by drawing closer to you.*
- *Give us, we pray, that insight which will enable us, in our own practice, to establish icons of the one holy catholic and apostolic church, so that we may be reminded continually that every tradition is imperfect and needs to be offered to you for cleansing and renewal*
      and that in Jesus Christ we have one Lord and Master
      in whom we are made sisters and brothers.

And to you Father, Son and Holy Spirit, be all glory, honour,
dominion and power, throughout the ages and for ever and ever.
                                                              Amen.

4

FAITH'S TESTING

Troubles and testing
End-game

PRACTICAL THEOLOGY

IN Lima, Peru, Sra. Valenzuela shared with me the experience of a member of a consultation for which she was then responsible, who came from her own native Chile. It made the point that if human beings are called 'to pray and not to faint' (Luke 18: 1) they are also called to see that prayer is not made a substitute for action.

In North Chile a drought had occurred which looked as if it would never end. The fields dried up. The cattle began to die. The people prayed for rain: but week after week passed with no relief. They just held on, feeling helpless, unable to provide enough food to save the cattle, idling away each day.

Then they came to themselves. 'Here we are,' they said, 'calling ourselves Christians and letting ourselves be beaten by circumstances. What should we do to show that we continue to hope in God?'

They talked it through and came to two main decisions.

Instead of allowing cattle to die off haphazardly, they allocated the food so that breeding pairs were preserved.

They could not plant crops so they constructed a much-needed road.

When the rains came they were able to build up the herd again and to tackle their farming more efficiently thanks to the road.

REFLECTION

*The biblical understanding of 'patience' is not just 'hanging on grimly,
regardless'. It has in it a recognition of the reality of suffering. It
contains also an encouragement to persist, whatever the odds. But
there is more to it: all this comes in a context of hope. The persistence
will be justified in the end! Even if one is thwarted again and again,
God will see to it that there is an eventual resolution. We are not
guaranteed that that will come this side of our death. But we are
guaranteed that it will come and will reward the investment of will
and energy, which we offer.*

I call it 'the Nelson Mandela factor'.

PRAYER

Father, Son and Holy Spirit,

> *What anguish you must have endured throughout history, as
human beings in whom you trusted failed you again and again; yet
you persisted with us, refusing any alterative way than that which
would make us your partners in the struggle for a new world.*

> > *We bless you for that trust.*

> > *We bless you for people like Mandela who endure the harshest
of circumstances and, year after weary year, refuse to lose
hope.*

> > *We bless you for those who face natural disasters with a deter-
mination to make the most of what is still left and build on
that.*

> > *We bless you that you have made us for yourself and that you
will never give us up.*

> > *We ask you that you enable us 'to run with patience the race
which is set before us, looking to Jesus, the author and finisher
of our faith'. Amen.*

AT THE END OF ONE'S TETHER

WORK for the World Council of Churches had daunting aspects. To a large extent the way in which one's mandate had to be tackled was left to oneself. At times I felt as if I was dropping small pebbles into a vast, still sea in the hope that at least a small ripple might be produced on an unknown distant shore.

For the 'Laity and Studies' project I had an excellent senior colleague in Ralph Young. Responsibility for tourism questions had been added. Then the Director of the Unit took ill. I was asked to take over the 'Participation in Change' programme (one of five major programmes decided on at the Uppsala Assembly) in addition to 'Laity' and 'Tourism' concerns. The total demand on my resources was high. Life began to lose focus. I found my grasp on it loosening. Worrying signs became apparent.

It was then that God's grace came to my rescue.

I argued with myself: a nervous breakdown would do nothing but harm to Margaret, the family, the World Council of Churches and myself. Avoiding action was called for.

My desk had six drawers, three on each side. I spread out all the requirements asked of me on the desktop. Into the first drawer went what I thought I could manage easily, into the next what I could tackle without too much difficulty and so on till the last drawer contained work which I judged I would not be likely ever to get round to.

I dealt with just one drawer at a time. The threat of breakdown disappeared.

REFLECTION

Lord, all my longing is known to you
my sighing is not hidden from you.
My heart throbs, my strength fails me
as for the light of my eyes – it also has gone from me.
Do not forsake me, O Lord,
O my God be not far from me:
make haste to help me O Lord, my salvation.

~ Psalm 38: 9, 10, 21, 22 ~

PRAYER

Lord God,
There are times in life when we do not know how to cope. The
ability to manage life slips from our hands. We get paralysed, do not
know where to turn, and our heart fails us.
If, then, we seek your face, there often seems to be no one there; it
is as if we had never prayed, never shown confidence in your saving
power; life goes on and buries us under its burdens.
But with you there is mercy.
You do not yield your help easily, but test our resilience, that we
might learn to persist, not just at one special time but over a lifetime
learning to handle crises, using the gifts with which you have endowed
us.
Then – you show us a way which can put an end to our fears,
some footholds which will allow us to climb out of the pit into which
we have fallen.
You still call on our initiative, our energies, our imagination; you
still add the requirement that we love ourselves and honour our own
abilities: then, together with you, we discover how to manage life.
This is the Lord's doing and it is marvellous in our eyes:
Thanks be to God. Amen.

IN NO-MAN'S LAND

THE No-Man's Land between Romania and Hungary was creepy. Margaret and I felt ill at ease as we crossed it. We had no idea that we would have to do so.

We were returning home from a conference at Poiana Brasov, Romania. Couchettes had been booked. But when we boarded the train we found them already occupied by people who menaced us when we tried to claim them. The attendant merely shrugged when we showed him our tickets – he had probably been bribed at Bucharest to turn a blind eye. Eventually an inspector opened a locked compartment which allowed us to stretch out.

Around five in the morning, we were awoken for passport examination. Some urgent information in Romanian, which we did not understand, was transmitted to us. We settled down again. Not long after, we stopped at a frontier station. We were unceremoniously dumped on a platform. The train continued on its way.

We could not make out what was amiss. In the languages which we had between us we enquired of the other waiting passengers, without success. Then, about half-seven, the assistant stationmaster arrived. He spoke French and was able to tell us that our visa, written in Hungarian, was a one-entry one when we had thought it provided for multiple entry. He advised us to take a train back to a certain station and there transfer to another train which could take us to a frontier post. There new visas could be bought. I had spare passport photos with me and had retained enough Romanian money to pay for tickets, so we set off. We were assured that there would be a bus or taxi to take us and our baggage across the five kilometres of frontier territory.

There was no taxi and no bus. We covered that weird no-man's land on foot, humping our baggage. At the other side we had to queue up behind a car, a public transport, then two more cars to be dealt with. We got the visa. A waiting train took us to Budapest and our flight home. But it was touch and go.

REFLECTION

Reflect on what it must be like to be a stranger, a refugee, an alien, a migrant in much more serious circumstances than Margaret and I ever encountered: confused for want of knowledge of languages, lacking the required identity documents, at the mercy of authorities who may interpret strictly the letter of the law or draw on its worst features: exposed and vulnerable, not knowing what a day will bring forth. Remember Leviticus 19: 33, 34 – 'If a stranger live with you in your land, do not ill-treat him. You must count him as one of your own countrymen and love him as yourself; for you were once strangers in Egypt. I am the Lord your God.'

'You were once strangers.' In every nation there are dwellers in the land who came from other countries which were torn by racism and war, or came in the wake of conquering armies. As generations pass they consider themselves to be natives, and others who seek entry to be intruders. Let us remember the melee of circumstance which made us a people and the great variety of racial blood which intermingles in every national community.

Pray that, as ancestors of yours found place and habitation in your own territory though they came as strangers, generosity may be shown to strangers by you and yours today.

'I am the Lord your God.' The ultimate reason for making room for strangers and giving them a welcome is that the earth is not ours. 'The earth is the Lord's and the fullness thereof.' It is given to provide habitation and sustenance for the whole human family.

In the light of this, examine your own government's immigration policies and pray and act with others to remedy deficiencies.

PRAYER

Lord of all life, we bring you those who are rebuffed in the society in which they seek refuge. Enable us by laws and personal friendship to overcome racial barriers which inhibit the construction of true and new community.

We ask it in Jesus' name. Amen.

THE IMPACT OF EVENTS

THE daughter of Brown the Fishmonger in Rosyth was an artist of quality. We value a painting of flowers which she had given us on our departure from the parish. She made fresh contact later, with the following request. She wanted to enter a portrait for the annual Women's Portraiture Exhibition in Edinburgh. Would I be prepared to sit for her?

We arranged about eight or ten sittings. It was agreed that I should not see the painting in its early stages. She would let me look at her work at the stage which she thought appropriate.

At first she seemed to be on song, pleased with progress. One day all that changed. She became disturbed. Her eyes went anxiously back and forth between myself and the canvas. She struggled to finish the sitting – and did so with relief as if she hoped that another day might show a problem disposed of. But it was not to be. She tried, tried again, looking at me from different angles. Finally she threw down her brushes and blurted out, 'I can't paint you – you're not the man I started with'. At that point she showed her canvas to the family. The strained, lined face seemed to them to be that of a stranger.

We agreed on a break, a fresh start, further sittings. The portrait was accepted and exhibited. But it did not have in it an insight which she was on the point of catching. For we looked back at dates and events. The change in my bearing coincided with the invasion of Czechoslovakia by USSR troops. The sorrow of that had penetrated and changed me.

REFLECTION

Joyce Cairns, portrait artist, was asked by me to make a head-and-shoulders' drawing as a family gift. She agreed but asked that she might also produce photographs. 'I think you will find that it is photographs, not drawings, which families really want. For a drawing, an artist fastens on an aspect of the sitter's character and lets the work flow from that. What families want is rather a representational image.'

As it turned out, she was right.

PRAYER

God the Lord of all,
        By your will we bear a family likeness to yourself.
You have given gifts to human beings to explore that likeness, showing up particularities and peculiarities, good and bad. Artists, dramatists, dancers, musicians, athletes have revealed your glory expressed in human form; and also seamy or strange aspects to which humanity is heir.
        We give thanks to you for those who use all the senses to appeal to all the senses, lifting the veil on truth – so that we better appreciate what stuff we are made of: for those
        who look into their own souls with the unblinking integrity of a Rembrandt;
        who expose human cruelty as 'Guernica' does;
        who explore new rhythms of life as did the founders of jazz;
        who let human sin be exposed as do Arthur Miller's dramas;
        who show grace and power combined on the track or field.
Lord God, save us from shielding ourselves from reality when its exposure may enable us to reckon both with our defects and with the promise of our lives:
        for then we may be freed to grow up into the stature and fullness of Jesus Christ
                for whom be glory for ever. Amen.

RISKS FOR PEACE

WHEN under the leadership of Roy Davey, there was a movement in Northern Ireland to establish a Centre of Reconciliation to help overcome Protestant/Roman Catholic divides, the Iona Community was asked to appoint someone to participate in the decisive meeting. It was thought that the Community might have relevant experience which could be contributed. I was given the assignment. From that meeting Corrymeela was launched.

The overcoming of fear can be illustrated by the following account coming from the Shankill and Falls Adventure Youth Work Camp held in the summer of 1970:

'A story illustrates the aspect of reconciliation in our project. On the Friday after the Adventure Camp, we visited St John's Youth Club on the Falls Road (Catholic) to meet the boys from the camp. They were very happy to meet us, and when we were leaving to go across the Peace Line to meet the Protestant boys, six of them wanted to come with us. We told them that it was dangerous, but the boys would be safe as long as no one overheard us saying their names (*eg* Michael and Patrick – which are regarded as Catholic names). Despite the fact that they were scared, they came with us. We passed safely through the gap in the Peace Line, although some of us noticed that the soldiers on guard, with their rifles at the ready, were a little nervous about us. We all met the Protestant boys at their Youth Club on the Shankill Road, and later noticed four of them, two Catholic and two Protestant, playing table tennis together. The following day, some of the Catholic boys returned to help decorate the club.

'Each time, they risked being beaten up to come with us, a sign that courage and friendship had in this situation overcome fear and division.'

PRAYER

God of peace and lover of concord,

*We confess, in past history, that we have treated others in a way
which dishonours your name. Even those who belong to the same
faith have been dealt with as enemies. We have looked for the worst
in them and have highlighted it. We have exaggerated the credibility
of our own positions. Followers who were meant to form one
company striving against sin have occupied hostile camps.*

We have failed you and let humanity down.

*How can you forgive us, you who see the hatred and bloodshed
generated through the centuries, concealing your nature and defiling
your name?*

*How can you put up with us who continually promise better and
then fall down on that promise?*

We give you thanks for Jesus Christ our Lord:

that he knows what it is like to have a nature like ours,

*that it was in accepting such a nature that he wrought our
    redemption,*

*that he is lord of history, able to deal with the foul deeds of the
    past,*

that in him we can be cleansed utterly and given a fresh start.

*We give you thanks for young people who take courageous steps to
restore broken links of friendship, afraid of the danger, yet facing it;*

for women who lead peace initiatives;

*for politicians who genuinely seek to overcome
    the divisions of history.*

Without you we would be lost. With you, all things are possible.

Hear us and help us we humbly beseech you, O Lord. Amen.

WORK WHILE IT IS DAY

WE had returned to Scotland on retirement.

When it proved possible to get things straight and I got some space, I said, 'I'll look up Winifred' – Winifred Rushforth of the Davidson Clinic, Wellspring and a host of other creative ventures.

She was over 90 at that time. She greeted me warmly but without surprise. 'I was told that I would not be allowed to die without seeing you again,' she said. Yet over the 15 months or so since our return to Scotland she had not attempted to contact me. She had been told she would see me. She just waited calmly for that to take place.

She spoke to me of initiatives, such as the founding of Wellspring, which she said we had invented and worked out together at Scottish Churches' House during the 1960s. I am sure she gave me more credit than I was due – as I remember it, these were her own ventures. Her memory was simply burnished by generosity.

Some time later I took Margaret to see her. She was delighted. In particular she wanted to share with us a recent experience. 'I was feeling close to my husband' – he had died many years previously – 'closer than I had been for a long time. I confess I was trading on that a bit. Then he pulled me up sharp: "Winifred," he said, "you are spending time and energy seeking to be near me. You have a job to do before you die – you know what it is and I know what it is. If you would only give full attention to the job and get it done, we would be together again all the sooner".'

Not long after, Winifred finished her life-work and joined him.

PRAYER

Lord God,
mysteriously you join, mysteriously you separate lives.
We are given to one another for a time. In that time we might seem
to become inseparable. We share so deeply – thoughts, ideas, respon-
sibilities, pleasures, pains. We become closely knit in life.

Then we are separated, and go to our long home. The mourners go
about the streets. Dust returns to the earth and breath returns to you
who gave it.* The world shifts off its axis, and life is never the same
again. Why, Lord God, why?

Why the deep belonging and then the parting?

Can it be that to have experienced a loving relationship and to
have lost it (at least as it was) is to be made a more rounded and
complete human being – and found to be so when others turn for
help in their need?

Open our eyes to your grace at work in the world, Lord God.

Can it be that there are assignments to undertake which may be
better tackled by one partner – now released to give all his/her energy
to the task – the role of the other partner being to cheer on the one
who is left and lend added strength from a different sphere?

Open our eyes to your grace at work in the world, Lord God.

Or can it be that, as Jesus was exposed to all the risks of human
living, so are we? Any one of us may be tortured and killed by human
intent, or be the victim of an accident, or be fatally assailed by disease
or be caught in a natural calamity, without you intervening

then what you do is take the worst which can happen to us, and
change weeping into joy by your creative touch?

Open our eyes to your grace at work in the world, Lord God.

[*Ecclesiastes 12: 5-7.]

LAST MESSAGE

ON one occasion, 'I can't think what to give you,' said Margaret when a birthday or Christmas loomed. So I suggested a New English Bible, a zipped edition which I could take on my travels. I duly got my present, but protested she had not inscribed it. 'I couldn't think what to say.'

Every third year or so thereafter I would remind her of her omission, without result. Nine years went by.

When we were in Bossey, the World Council of Churches Study Centre, and the second cancer which proved fatal attacked her, we were together in our room. To get her back home immediately I had to make a main contribution to the conference the next morning (she was not fit to take part in our planned double act); and had to concentrate to get in hand material which I had not expected to put in order until nearer the end of that week. She was lying in bed, fighting the cancer, when she said quietly, 'I have inscribed the bible'.

'Great!' I answered, and bent again to the work. Only afterwards did it strike me that she said it as if she meant it to stay at the back of my mind, not get immediate attention.

Three months after her death I was in Holland for a conference.

I opened the bible. There was her last message to me:

> To Dearest Ian
> in gratitude for love &
> companionship over so many
> happy years.
> Margaret.

How thoughtful. How heart-warming. How like Margaret.

REFLECTION

Love between people is full of the mystery of God's giving.
Life comes to us unasked: we do not decide when or where.
Paths which might have diverged, cross.
Mysterious forces draw us to one another.
Friendships are made and may deepen into love.
'This is the Lord's doing and it is marvellous in our eyes.'
And this is part of the redemption of the whole creation which looks
with expectation to see whether humans will so live in love that they
are worthy of being called children of God. The arrival of that time will
trigger the release of everything in creation into completeness of life.
'Faith, hope and love abide, these three,
and the greatest of these is love.'

PRAYER

Holy Trinity, you are a Trinity of love. We can love only because you
share your life with us. May our love be of that unselfish, self-sacri-
ficing kind which is rooted in your life and bears fruit in the world.

We give thanks for poets who can put into words experiences
which would seem to defy words; and for humble folk who are poets
without knowing it.

We pray for people who have longed to be personally, particularly
loved and have never known that grace: and we give thanks for those
who provide friendship and a loving embrace for the ones who thus
miss out.

We pray for those trapped in loveless and unsustainable partner-
ships, and for children who suffer whether the partners stay together
or separate.

We pray for one-parent families struggling against the odds; that
children may have love expressed both in the provision of food and
clothing and in hugs.

We give thanks for language which conveys deep commitment;
and ask your grace for the tongue-tied who have the commitment but
cannot find words for it.

Trinity of love, help our weakness; grant us love like yours. Amen.

REASSURANCE

WHEN Margaret died, I was specially concerned for a member of the congregation of Rosyth Parish Church, where we had earlier served for twelve years. Robina Cameron had suffered some facial disfigurement as a result of tuberculosis when she was a young girl. She was rather shy. Margaret's friendship meant a great deal to her. She was one of those who made the faces of our family brighten when they heard we were both to be out of an evening. 'Goody!' was the children's response. 'Will the sitter-in be Mary or Bina?' Now she was in her eighties and frail.

Fearing that she would be taking Margaret's death very sorely, I phoned the day after the funeral and asked whether I could come and rehearse to her all that had happened. She welcomed this. I lost no time in going.

I found her composed and tranquil. I shared the details. She thanked me; then she said she had something to share in return.

She was not usually fit enough to go to communion services in the parish kirk. But that Ascension Day she had felt impelled to go. During the service, Margaret had appeared to her three times. She was at no greater distance than the pew in front. Everything else in the church became indistinct compared with the vividness of that presence. Margaret looked on her with loving concern. The third appearance was a withdrawing one. It was clearly also a farewell. Bina was flooded with peace.

Trust Margaret to upstage me at the loving game!

REFLECTION

'I believe in the resurrection of the body.'

The body is our mark of identity. When Margaret appeared to Bina after death, she was still Margaret, not some unrecognisable spectre.

On one occasion when I saw her in a dream, she was not quite as she had been, but I knew it was her. I remember saying to myself, still in the dream, 'When Jesus appeared to his disciples they did not at first recognise him, and only later knew it was him. The resurrection makes us genuinely, recognisably ourselves, but changed!'

PRAYER

Lord God, how gracious you are.

Even in the resurrection you accept us as recognisably ourselves.

You do not want to slough off all that we have been, though so much of it has been offensive to you. You forgive it and transform it and make it sound out your praise. We who have made ourselves unacceptable in your sight are accepted in our entirety 'just as we are, your own to be'.

You transform our lives – yet we can recognise one another in the resurrection and rejoice in one another again and knit up life after long parting.

In the great host around the throne, which no one can number, we can hold hands once more, hug one another once more. The praise of our lips will not be praise in general. It will be formed from particular lives lifted up and made an offering, joined with other particular lives which make up that throng.

Let all the people say 'Amen'.